# SIX TENNYSON ESSAYS

# SIX TENNYSON ESSAYS

BY

SIR CHARLES TENNYSON

ROWMAN AND LITTLEFIELD
TOTOWA, NEW JERSEY

THIS EDITION FIRST PUBLISHED IN THE UNITED STATES 1972
*by Rowman and Littlefield, Totowa, New Jersey*

ISBN 0 87471 072 3

FIRST PUBLISHED 1954
*by Cassell & Co. Ltd., London*



PRINTED IN GREAT BRITAIN
by Scolar Press Ltd.,
Menston, Yorkshire, U.K.

# SIX TENNYSON ESSAYS

# Six Tennyson Essays

by

CHARLES TENNYSON

*Author of 'Life's all a Fragment'*

CASSELL & CO LTD

LONDON

CASSELL & CO LTD
37/38 St. Andrew's Hill, Queen Victoria Street
London, E.C.4

*and at*

31/34 George IV Bridge, Edinburgh
210 Queen Street, Melbourne
26/30 Clarence Street, Sydney
Haddon Hall, City Road, Auckland, N.Z.
1068 Broadview Avenue, Toronto 6
420 West 45th Street, New York 36
Avenida 9 de Julho 1138, São Paulo
Galeria Güemes, Escritorio 518/520 Florida 165, Buenos Aires
Haroon Chambers, South Napier Road, Karachi
15 Graham Road, Ballard Estate, Bombay 1
17 Central Avenue P.O. Dharamtala, Calcutta
P.O. Box 275, Cape Town
P.O. Box 1386, Salisbury, S. Rhodesia
P.O. Box 959, Accra, Gold Coast
25 rue Henri Barbusse, Paris 5e
Islands Brygge 5, Copenhagen


*First published* 1954

Set in 12pt. Bembo type and
printed in Great Britain by
T. and A. Constable Ltd., Hopetoun Street, Edinburgh
F. 1253

TO

FRYN TENNYSON JESSE

WITH LOVE AND ADMIRATION

# PREFACE

IN THESE ESSAYS I have tried to deal with aspects of Tennyson's poetry which seem hitherto to have received inadequate consideration. The first contains a study of the humorous element in his work, which has been very little noticed by critics, with the honourable exception of that stalwart Tennysonian, Mr. John Betjemann. A good deal has been written about the Poet's political and religious views, but little attempt has been made to relate these to contemporary events and controversies, without which they cannot be fully understood or estimated. In my second and third essays I have tried to include purely objective studies of these two aspects of Tennyson's poetry. The fourth essay contains a more detailed analysis of his prosody and metrical achievement than has, I think, yet been attempted. The fifth, which is based on the study of early MSS. of the *Idylls of the King*, is republished from *The Cornhill Magazine* by kind permission of the proprietors, and I have added to it a note on Tennyson's ability as a story-teller. The last essay, which is largely based on the old phonograph records made by Edison in 1889, deals with the reading of his poems aloud. I hope that the six essays together may give some idea, however inadequate, of the range, depth and complexity of the creative work of a great poet.

# CONTENTS

# I

# *Tennyson as a Humorist*

ON A FIRST HEARING probably most people would reject with amazement the suggestion that Tennyson is the most humorous of all the great English poets since Chaucer, excepting, of course—as one always has to except from such generalizations—Shakespeare. Yet I think the claim can be made good. That he himself was a great humorist is plain to any reader of Fitzgerald's letters or Allingham's diary. It is recorded that at Cambridge he would make his friends laugh till they rolled off their seats with his readings from Rabelais; and forty years later he himself laughed till the tears came when reading Tom Hood's *Whims and Oddities* to the boys at Marlborough. He was a famous *raconteur*, with an excellent gift of mimicry, and in later life often spoke of making a collection of the world's hundred best anecdotes, which, he said—no doubt not altogether seriously—would be of more value than all the rest of his works put together. Frederick Locker, himself a delightful humorist, closed his description of a tour which he and the poet made in Switzerland with the surprising, but no doubt perfectly sincere ejaculation, 'Does anyone make one laugh like Alfred Tennyson?' Tennyson himself considered humour one of the most valuable human qualities, and a letter to his future wife, written when he was just over thirty, contains a striking expression of this view.

> I cannot tell thee how [highly] I rate this faculty which is generally most fruitful in the highest and most solemn human spirits. Dante is full of it. Shakespeare, Cervantes and almost all the greatest, have been pregnant with this glorious power. Thou wilt find it even in the gospel of Christ.

To many this will seem an exaggerated claim, but Tennyson had special reason to make it, for without his own sense of humour he would, I believe, scarcely have maintained his sanity through the corroding miseries and the cruel shocks and disappointments of his youth and early manhood.

It is surprising, therefore, that the humorous element in his work should have been so consistently overlooked. The main cause of this has, I believe, been the extraordinary range and variety of his achievement. It was difficult to think of the author of *In Memoriam* and (for different reasons) 'The May Queen' as a humorist, and readers and critics have tended to concentrate both their approval and disapproval on what they considered more important aspects of his poetry. A subsidiary cause has been what one may call the Bardic legend about Tennyson, encouraged by the adoration of his family and friends, and intensified by the splendour of his personal appearance and the seclusion of his life. Something may also be due to the fact that the humorous element hardly appeared in his work until the publication, in his thirty-third year, of the second of his famous volumes of 1842. Dates of publication are, however, often very misleading as evidence, and Tennyson's humorous faculty was in reality a very early development.

One of the most deliberately and effectively humorous works that he ever produced was not published until 1930—thirty-eight years after his death and one hundred and seven years after it had been written. This was the now famous blank-verse comedy, *The Devil and The Lady*, which he wrote when only fourteen years old. It shows that even at that age Tennyson had an exuberant—and at times subtle—sense of humour and a sure instinct, nourished on a precocious study of the Elizabethan and Jacobean drama, for the expression of this in verse. The play tells the story of an aged magician (Magus) who, being called away suddenly upon some mystic errand, summons up the Devil and entrusts him with the task of looking after his young wife, Amoret, in his absence. The Devil packs Amoret off to bed, disguises himself in her clothes and then admits her lovers (a lawyer, a soldier, a sailor, an apothecary, an astronomer and a monk), to Magus's cottage, where he diverts himself with them until her husband returns. The choice of such a theme (a singular one for the fourteen-year-old son of a country parson, even in the reign of George IV) shows that at fourteen Tennyson already had a sure grasp of the principle on which all humour is said to be based—that of contrast or incongruity.

From this point of view the plot is a brilliant comic invention. The contrast between the prosy, idealistic old wizard and his wanton young wife; the Devil's embarrassment at the charge entrusted to him; the lady's horror and amazement when she finds that the father of Evil is taking his duties conscientiously; that 'petticoated solecism', as the wizard calls him, the disguised Devil, who has 'girdled his brown sides' and 'propped his monstrous vertebrae with stays', and the absurdities of the deluded suitors, who make love and quarrel each of them in the jargon of his profession, provide the true stuff of robust comedy. The following extracts from the scenes in which Magus takes leave of his young wife and she finds herself confronted with the Devil, will give some idea of the gusto with which the young author carried out his invention, and of his ability to adapt language and rhythms to the expression of his comic ideas:

MAGUS: And hark ye, Amoret, one word of counsel!
Close thou thy casement early, nor look down
At sound of querulous serenade or flute
Wooing the dewy wings o' th' midnight air. . . .
Regard not thou the glancing of the eye—
The pressure of the hand—the easy lapse
Of honey'd words from amatory lips—
All this regard not—Now farewell; may Heaven
And the good Saints protect thee! (*Going*

AMORET: The like wish
Attend thee on thy way!

MAGUS (*returning*): If I have said
Ought roughly or in anger—

AMORET: Think not of it!
Once more farewell—

MAGUS: Farewell, my own good Amoret,
And if my humour should sometimes show testy
Impute it all unto the love I bear thee,
Which effervesceth of its own intensity,
And oftentimes mounts upward and boils over
Because of its own fervour. (*Exit*

AMORET (*runs to the wings and shakes her fist after him*): Go thy ways!
Thou yellowest leaf on Autumn's wither'd tree!
Thou sickliest ear of all the sheaf! thou clod!
Thou fireless mixture of Earth's coldest clay!
Thou crazy dotard, crusted o'er with age
As thick as ice upon a standing pool!
Thou shrunken, sapless, wizen Grasshopper,
Consuming the green promise of my youth!
Go, get thee gone, and evil winds attend thee. . . .
Why was I link'd with such a frowzy mate,
With such a fusty partner of my days?

SCENE V (*Enter Devil*

(AMORET *shrieks, covers her face with her hand and runs to the door.* DEVIL *brings her back and forces her into a chair.*)

DEVIL: Madam! What's this? What? Railing? Fie! for shame!
(Nay, sit you still and hear me.) Think you then
To play Xantippe with impunity,
Who gave her philosophical old spouse
So choice and delicate a water bath
To whet his appetite one frosty morning
Before his breakfast? Do you hearken to me?

AMORET: Ye saints defend me—I shall die with terror.

DEVIL: How now, my dainty one, my delicate ward,
My pretty piece of frail mortality.
Where think you is the rendezvous of Saints,
Where their celestial club-room, that you make
A fretwork argent of your snowy fingers,
And cast your jetty pupils up on high
Until the blank, unanimated white
Usurps the field of vision?
A most unphilosophical conclusion!
Point thy hands downward, turn thine eyes to the floor!
There is a Heaven beneath this Earth as fair
As that which roofs it here.
Dost think that Heaven is local, and not rather

The omnipresence of the glorified
And liberated Spirit—the expansion
Of man's depress'd and fetter'd faculties
Into omniscience? . . .

AMORET: I know not whence thou comest,
Nor who thou art, nor what thy message here,
Nor how I may exorcise thee, or drive
Thy troubled spirit to its biding-place.
If there be ought of pity in thy soul,
I do beseech thee leave me to my thoughts
And solitude.

DEVIL: Thoughts! Thoughts! what thoughts are thine
But evil and dishonour?

AMORET: Nay, I'll kneel
And pray thee to depart.

DEVIL: Out on thee, woman!
Devils are faithful to their trust.

AMORET: Alas!
Am I entrusted then to thee?

DEVIL: Dost weep?
Is that a tear which stains thy cheek? Nay—now
It quivers at the tip-end of thy nose
Which makes it somewhat dubious from which feature
It first had issue.

AMORET: I conjure thee—

DEVIL: Tears!
The rain of sentiment, the dews of feeling,
The beads of sensibility!
They are the coinage of a single wish.
I know that ye can summon them at will.
They are a woman's weapons, sword and shield,
Wherewith she braves remonstrance and breaks hearts—
Those faithful sluices never are drawn dry. . . .
What! more! I know ye can command them, woman,

Even to the precise number, ten or twenty,
As suits occasion—
More yet? Methinks the cavity o' thy skull
Is brine i' th' room o' brains.

AMORET: I pray thee—

DEVIL: Get thee to bed—yet stay—but one word more—
Let there be no somnambulations,
No colloquy of soft-tongued whisperings
Like the low hum of the delighted bee
I' th' calyx of a lily—no kerchief-waving!
No footfalls i' th' still night! Lie quietly!
Without the movement of one naughty muscle. . . .
I know ye are perverse, and ever wish,
Maugre my wholesome admonitions,
To run obliquely like the bishop at chess,
But I'll cry 'check' to ye, I warrant ye
I'll prove a 'stalemate' to ye.

AMORET (*half-aside*): In all conscience
My mate is stale enough.

The years that followed the composition of *The Devil and the Lady* were for Tennyson years of intense mental development and intense suffering, owing to the disastrous condition of affairs at Somersby Rectory. It is, therefore, not surprising that the poems he wrote before going up to Cambridge were either (like his contributions to *Poems by Two Brothers*) conventional exercises in the popular poetic styles of the day, or agonized attempts at self-expression, such as some of those included in the *Unpublished Early Poems*, issued in 1931. With Cambridge there began a new phase, which again was not favourable to humorous treatment. Trinity and friendship with the brilliant young men of 'The Apostles' opened to the shy, introspective boy from the lonely hamlet in the Wolds a world of new ideas and aspirations, and made him realize unsuspected potentialities in his own nature. The call to explore these was urgent and for the time overwhelming. Consequently there is no definitely humorous poem in the volumes Tennyson published in 1830 and 1832, although here and there the reader is conscious that the spirit of humour is hovering in the background—as, for example, in the grim description of a Cambridge prig:

*He spake of beauty, that the dull*
*Saw no divinity in grass,*
*Life in dead stones, or spirit in air;*
*Then looking as 'twere in a glass,*
*He smooth'd his chin and sleek'd his hair,*
*And said the earth was beautiful.*

*He spake of virtue: not the gods*
*More purely, when they wish to charm*
*Pallas and Juno sitting by,*
*And with a sweeping of the arm,*
*And a lack-lustre dead blue eye,*
*Devolved his rounded periods.*

*With lips depress'd as he were meek,*
*Himself unto himself he sold,*
*Upon himself himself did feed,*
*Quiet, dispassionate, and cold,*
*And other than his form of creed,*
*With chisell'd features clear and sleek.*

There is a background of humour, too, in *Recollections of the Arabian Nights*—particularly in the description of the good Haroun Alraschid seated by the sleeping Persian beauty—

*. . . his deep eye laughter-stirred*
*With merriment of kingly pride*

and in the poems addressed to 'Lilian', 'Adeline', 'Margaret', 'Kate' and other real or imaginary maidens. The humorous element is strongest in one of the best of these works, which was never published until it appeared in *Unpublished Early Poems.*

### *Lisette*

*My light Lisette*
*Is grave and shrewd,*
*And half a prude,*
*And half coquette,*
*So staid and set,*
*So terse and trim,*
*So arch and prim*
*Is my Lisette.*

*A something settled and precise*
*Hath made a home in both the eyes*
*Of my Lisette,*
*Lives in the little wilful hands,*
*The little foot that glides and flits,*
*Braced with dark silken sandal-bands,*
*Even in the coxcomb parrokette*
*That on the drooping shoulder sits*
*Of trim Lisette.*

*The measured motion of the blood;*
*The words, where each one tells,*
*Too logical for womanhood,*
*Brief changes rung on silver bells;*
*The cheek with health's close kisses warm,*
*The finished form so light;*
*Such fullness in a little form*
*As satisfies the sight.*

*The bodice fitted so exact;*
*The nutbrown tress so crisply curled,*
*And the whole woman so compact,*
*Her match is nowhere in the world;*
*Such knowledge of the modes of life,*
*And household order such,*
*As might create a perfect wife,*
*Not careful overmuch;*

*All these so moved me*
*When we met,*
*I would she loved me,*
*Trim Lisette.*

*What if to-morrow morn I go,*
*And in an accent clipt and clear*
*Say some three words within her ear,*
*I think she would not answer 'No.'*
*But by the ribbon in her hair,*
*And those untasted lips, I swear,*
*I keep some little doubt as yet;*
*With such an eye*
*So grave and sly*
*Looks my Lisette.*
*What words may show*
*The 'Yes'—the 'No'—*
*Of trim Lisette?*
*The doubt is less*
*Since last we met,*
*Let it be 'Yes',*'
*My sweet Lisette.*

Among all the surviving poems of these years there is only one written with an entirely humorous intention—the lines 'To a Portrait', first printed in *Unpublished Early Poems*. This was clearly written by Tennyson as an exercise in the manner of Praed, since the first two lines are identical with Praed's verses 'To the Portrait of a Lady in the Exhibition of the Royal Academy', published in 1831, though the two poems have no resemblance after the fourth line, except metrically.

Overleaf are Tennyson's lines in metre, differing from Praed's poem—which will be found on p. 155 of the Second Volume of the Collected Edition issued by Moxon—only in having one foot, of two syllables, less in the third line of the stanza.

*Lines*
*to the Picture of a Young Lady of Fashion*

*What are you, lady? Nought is here*
*To tell your name or story,*
*To claim for you our smile or tear,*
*To dub you Whig or Tory;*
*I don't suppose we ever met,*
*And how shall I discover*
*Where first you danced a minuet,*
*Or first deceived a lover?*

*Tell me what day the Post records*
*Your mother's silk and satin;*
*What night your father lulls the Lords*
*With little bits of Latin;*
*Who makes your shoes, whose skill designs*
*Your dairy or your grotto;*
*And in what page Debrett enshrines*
*Your pedigree and motto.*

*And do you sing or do you sigh?*
*And have you taste in bonnets?*
*And do you read philosophy?*
*Or do you publish sonnets?*
*And does your beauty fling away*
*The fetters Cupid forges?*
*Or—are you to be married, pray,*
*To-morrow at St. George's?*

*I ceased—methought the pencilled fan*
*Fluttered, or seemed to flutter—*
*Methought the painted lips began*
*Unearthly sounds to mutter, . . .*
*'I have no house, no ancestry,*
*No wealth, no reputation;*
*My name, fair sir, is "Nobody";*
*Am I not your relation?'*

Within a year of the publication of the volume of 1832 Arthur Hallam died and Tennyson, broken by his loss and depressed by the rancorous attacks of the critics on his first two volumes, published nothing more (except one or two brief lyrics in periodicals) until 1842, when he brought out two volumes, one containing a revised selection from his two earlier volumes and one composed entirely of new poems.

The latter volume showed a remarkable change of tone, which has not, I think, been sufficiently noticed—a marked increase of detachment and objectivity. The change was to some extent obscured by the inclusion in the book of a number of poems (some of them, like 'The Two Voices', and 'Break, Break, Break', intensely subjective), written just before or soon after the death of Hallam. However, even in some of these (for example, 'St. Simeon Stylites') the new note was discernible, largely through a greatly increased expression of the Poet's sense of humour. This showed itself in three entirely new types of poem—the *English Idyls*; poems in what has come to be called Tennyson's Horatian vein; and the two curious exercises in the macabre: 'St. Simeon Stylites' and 'The Vision of Sin'. The *Idyls* included 'The Gardener's Daughter', the Prologue and Epilogue to the 'Morte d'Arthur', 'Audley Court', and 'Walking to the Mail'. In them Tennyson added a new *genre* to English poetry, modelled on the pastoral poems of Theocritus, for Southey's *English Eclogues* are so featureless that they entirely fail to reproduce the effect of the Greek models. Tennyson's *Idyls* are little pictures of contemporary English life written with a classical economy of language and making their effect by their atmosphere, vivid charm and humorous detachment. 'The Gardener's Daughter', written in 1833, before Arthur Hallam's death, is the earliest and much the richest in texture of all the *Idyls*. It is an old man's reminiscence of his country courtship, half humorous and half regretful, written with all a young man's zest and exuberance, but less definitely humorous than the later *Idyls*. The lines that precede and succeed the 'Morte d'Arthur' give an English country-house setting to Tennyson's poetic version of Malory's story of King Arthur's death, to which they make an admirable foil, with their picture of the young men talking over the wassail-bowl on Christmas Eve after a day's skating. The parson Holmes—

*Taking wide and wider sweeps,*
*Now harping on the Church Commissioners,*
*Now hawking at geology and schism*

and settling down at last

*on the general decay of faith*
*Right thro' the world. . . .*

leads aptly and humorously up to the antique story, during the reading of which he falls fast asleep, and the Epilogue leaves the poet dreaming that—

*Arthur is come again, he cannot die.*
*. . . . . . . . . . . . . . . . . . . . . come*
*With all good things and war shall be no more.*

'Audley Court' describes two young men picnicking in the orchard of a Devonshire manor house on a summer evening, with

*a dusky loaf that smelt of home,*
*And half cut down, a pasty costly-made*
*Where quail and pigeon, lark and leveret lay,*
*Like fossils of the rock, with golden yolks*
*Imbedded and injellied; . . .*

There they talk old matters over:

*who was dead,*
*Who married, who was like to be, and how*
*The races went and who would rent the hall*

until they split upon the corn-laws:

*And come again together on the king*
*With heated faces. . . .*

Then, after an exchange of songs, they saunter home together beneath the crescent moon. 'Walking to the Mail' is equally slight—a dialogue between two friends strolling through the spring meadows to catch the mail coach. They gossip about the neighbours—the squire who,

*vex'd with a morbid devil in his blood*

and scared of Chartist agitators

*lest a cry*
*Should break his sleep by night, and his nice eyes*
*Should see the raw mechanic's bloody thumbs*
*Sweat on his blazon'd chairs*

has fled abroad, leaving behind his lady:

*A woman like a butt, and harsh as crabs*

whom he had married ten years since, when she was a sweet and simple cottager's daughter,

*A body slight and round and like a pear in growing. . . .*
*. . . and a skin*
*As clean and white as privet when it flowers.*

This gossip closes with a couple of anecdotes—one of Eton Boys who kept a stolen sow on the roof of Long Chamber till they had killed and eaten all her litter, when they returned the 'Niobe of Swine' 'unfarrow'd to her sty', and one of the haunted farmer who, to escape the ghost, packs up all his belongings and sets off in his waggon:

*. . . with his boy between his knees*
*His wife upon the tilt.*

'What! you're flitting?' says a friend who meets them on the road.

*'Yes, we're flitting,' says the ghost*
*(For they had packed the things among the beds)*
*'Oh well,' says he, 'you're flitting with us too.*
*John, turn the horses' heads and home again.'*

These early *Idyls*, for all their slightness, are vivid and full of charm. Tennyson improved on them considerably in two *Idyls* which were published respectively in 1851 and 1855—'Edwin Morris' and 'The Brook'. In the first, a middle-aged townsman recalls the

*. . . sweet, wild, fresh three quarters of a year,*
*The one oasis in the dust and drouth of City life*

spent with two friends at Llanberis, where he fell in love with Letty, the daughter of a millionaire living on an island in the middle of the lake. The close of the poem tells of the collapse of his love affair:

> *But, when the bracken rusted on their crags,*
> *My suit had wither'd, nipt to death by him*
> *That was a God, and is a lawyer's clerk,*
> *The rentroll Cupid of our rainy isles.*
> *'Tis true, we met; one hour I had, no more;*
> *She sent a note, the seal an* Elle vous suit,
> *The close, 'Your Letty, only yours;' and this*
> *Thrice underscored. The friendly mist of morn*
> *Clung to the lake. I boated over, ran*
> *My craft aground, and heard with beating heart*
> *The Sweet-Gale rustle round the shelving keel;*
> *And out I stept, and up I crept; she moved,*
> *Like Proserpine in Enna, gathering flowers;*
> *Then low and sweet I whistled thrice; and she,*
> *She turn'd, we closed, we kiss'd, swore faith, I breathed*
> *In some new planet; a silent cousin stole*
> *Upon us and departed: 'Leave,' she cried,*
> *'O leave me!' 'Never, dearest, never: here*
> *I brave the worst:' and while we stood like fools*
> *Embracing, all at once a score of pugs*
> *And poodles yell'd within, and out they came*
> *Trustees and Aunts and Uncles. 'What, with him!*
> *Go' (shrill'd the cotton-spinning chorus); 'him!'*
> *I choked. Again they shriek'd the burthen—'Him!'*
> *Again with hands of wild rejection—'Go!—*
> *Girl, get you in!' She went—and in one month*
> *They wedded her to sixty thousand pounds,*
> *To lands in Kent and messuages in York,*
> *And slight Sir Robert with his watery smile*
> *And educated whisker.*

'The Brook', which is generally mentioned only because of the charming, if rather facile, lyric which runs through it, is undoubtedly the strongest, as it is the longest, of the *Idyls*. Characteristic of its humour is the episode in which the Poet agrees to help the farmer's daughter to a quiet hour alone with her lover by allowing her garrulous old father, Philip Willows, to take him round the farm.

*'O Katie, what I suffer'd for your sake!*
*For in I went, and call'd old Philip out*
*To show the farm: full willingly he rose:*
*He led me thro' the short sweet-smelling lanes*
*Of his wheat-suburb, babbling as he went.*
*He praised his land, his horses, his machines;*
*He praised his ploughs, his cows, his hogs, his dogs;*
*He praised his hens, his geese, his guinea-hens;*
*His pigeons, who in session on their roofs*
*Approved him, bowing at their own deserts;*
*Then from the plaintive mother's teat he took*
*Her blind and shuddering puppies, naming each,*
*And naming those his friends, for whom they were:*
*Then crost the common into Darnley chase*
*To show Sir Arthur's deer. In copse and fern*
*Twinkled the innumerable ear and tail.*
*Then, seated on a serpent-rooted beech,*
*He pointed out a pasturing colt, and said:*
*"That was the four-year-old I sold the Squire."*
*And there he told a long long-winded tale*
*Of how the Squire had seen the colt at grass,*
*And how it was the thing his daughter wish'd,*
*And how he sent the bailiff to the farm*
*To learn the price, and what the price he ask'd,*
*And how the bailiff swore that he was mad,*
*But he stood firm; and so the matter hung;*
*He gave them line: and five days after that*
*He met the bailiff at the Golden Fleece,*
*Who then and there had offer'd something more,*
*But he stood firm; and so the matter hung;*
*He knew the man; the colt would fetch its price;*
*He gave them line; and how by chance at last*
*(It might be May or April, he forgot,*
*The last of April or the first of May)*
*He found the bailiff riding by the farm,*

*And, talking from the point, he drew him in,*
*And there he mellow'd all his heart with ale,*
*Until they closed a bargain, hand in hand.*
*Then, while I breathed in sight of haven, he,*
*Poor fellow, could he help it? recommenced,*
*And ran thro' all the coltish chronicle,*
*Wild Will, Black Bess, Tantivy, Tallyho,*
*Reform, White Rose, Bellerophon, the Jilt,*
*Arbaces, and Phenomenon, and the rest,*
*Till, not to die a listener, I arose,*
*And with me Philip, talking still; and so*
*We turn'd our foreheads from the falling sun,*
*And following our own shadows thrice as long*
*As when they follow'd us from Philip's door,*
*Arrived and found the sun of sweet content*
*Re-risen in Katie's eyes, and all things well.'*

'St. Simeon' and 'The Vision of Sin' are in a vein which Tennyson never repeated, although it was one familiar in his conversation. At Cambridge, for instance, he was famous for an imitation of Satan, as described in the fourth book of *Paradise Lost*, squatting, in the shape of a toad, 'close at the ear of Eve':

*. . . Endeavouring by his devilish arts to reach*
*The organs of her fancy. . . .*

and then, at a touch from the Archangel's spear, starting up in his own foul shape 'discovered and surprised'; and in later life he enjoyed the grimmest of jokes and would, for example, imitate a cannibal chief walking up and down to inspect a row of missionaries destined for the pot. Moreover, he had experimented with the macabre at a very early age, as is shown by a poem entitled 'The Coach of Death' (see *Memoir*, p. 23), which was written at about the same time as *The Devil and the Lady*—e.g. the following lines describing the Coach and its driver:

*Dark was the night, and loud the roar*
  *Of wind and mingled shower,*
*When there stood a dark coach at an Old Inn door*
  *At the solemn midnight hour. . . .*

*No sound of joy, no revelling tones*
*Of carouse were heard within:*
*But the rusty sign of a skull and cross-bones*
*Swung creaking before the Inn. . . .*

*Dimly the travellers look'd thro' the glooms,*
*Worn and wan was their gaze, I trow,*
*As the shrivell'd forms of the shadowy grooms*
*Yoked the skeleton horses to.*

*There came a gaunt man from the dark Inn door,*
*A dreadnought coat had he;*
*His bones crack'd loud, as he stept thro' the crowd,*
*And his boots creak'd heavily.*

*Before his eyes so grim and calm*
*The tingling blood grew chill,*
*As each put a farthing into his palm,*
*To drive them where he will.*

*His sockets were eyeless, but in them slept*
*A red infernal glow;*
*As the cockroach crept, and the white fly leapt*
*About his hairless brow.*

*They mounted slow in their long black cloaks,*
*The tears bedimm'd their sight;*
*The grim old coachee strode to the box*
*And the guard gasp'd out 'All's right.'*

'St. Simeon' and 'The Vision of Sin' make an extraordinary contrast to the *English Idyls*. The first, a monologue by a Syrian anchorite, who is said to have lived for thirty years entirely without shelter on the top of a tall pillar, was a favourite with the Poet, who would read it with grotesque grimness, often laughing aloud at its ferocious humours. Unfortunately one cannot do justice to it by quotation. Still stranger is 'The Vision of Sin', a fantasy which, I believe, was probably written, like 'St. Simeon', at the end of 1833 or soon after. In the closing section of this, the old cynic:

*. . . a gray and gap-toothed man as lean as death,*

who is carousing with the

*. . . slip-shod waiter, lank and sour*

at the ruined tavern on the heath and trying to wake in him some of the long-quenched fire of youth, evokes a vision of the old waiter's early loves.

*'Tell me tales of thy first love—*
*April hopes, the fools of chance;*
*Till the graves begin to move,*
*And the dead begin to dance.*

*'Trooping from their mouldy dens*
*The chap-fallen circle spreads;*
*Welcome, fellow-citizens,*
*Hollow hearts and empty heads!*

*'You are bones, and what of that?*
*Every face, however full,*
*Padded round with flesh and fat,*
*Is but modell'd on a skull.*

*'Death is king, and Vivat Rex!*
*Tread a measure on the stones,*
*Madam—if I know your sex,*
*From the fashion of your bones.*

*'No I cannot praise the fire*
*In your eye—nor yet your lip:*
*All the more do I admire*
*Joints of cunning workmanship.*

*'Lo! God's likeness—the ground-plan—*
*Neither modell'd, glazed, nor framed;*
*Buss me, thou rough sketch of man,*
*Far too naked to be shamed!'*

The Horatian vein, which appeared for the first time in the 1842 volume, was one which suited Tennyson extraordinarily well and which he used freely throughout his long life, though after 1842 generally in poems of sentiment rather than humour; for example, 'The Daisy', and the introductory lines to 'Tiresias' and 'The Progress of Spring'. An admirable example in this first series is 'Will Waterproof's Lyrical Monologue', in which the Poet pictures himself musing over a pint of port in the Cock Tavern in Fleet Street, and passing in review the failures and successes of his hitherto not very successful life. The last section will give an idea of the urbanity and neatness of this charming poem:

*Head-waiter of the chop-house here,*
*To which I most resort,*
*I too must part: I hold thee dear*
*For this good pint of port.*
*For this, thou shalt from all things suck*
*Marrow of mirth and laughter;*
*And wheresoe'er thou move, good luck*
*Shall fling her old shoe after.*

*But thou wilt never move from hence,*
*The sphere thy fate allots:*
*Thy latter days increased with pence*
*Go down among the pots;*
*Thou battenest by the greasy gleam*
*In haunts of hungry sinners,*
*Old boxes, larded with the steam*
*Of thirty thousand dinners.*

*We fret, we fume, would shift our skins,*
*Would quarrel with out lot;*
*Thy care is, under polish'd tins,*
*To serve the hot-and-hot;*
*To come and go, and come again,*
*Returning like the pewit,*
*And watch'd by silent gentlemen,*
*That trifle with the cruet.*

*Live long, ere from thy topmost head*
*The thick-set hazel dies;*
*Long, ere the hateful crow shall tread*
*The corners of thine eyes,*
*Live long, nor feel in head or chest*
*Our changeful equinoxes,*
*Till mellow Death, like some late guest,*
*Shall call thee from the boxes.*

*But when he calls, and thou shalt cease*
*To pace the gritted floor,*
*And, laying down an unctuous lease*
*Of life, shall earn no more;*
*No carved cross-bones, the types of Death,*
*Shall show thee past to Heaven:*
*But carved cross-pipes, and, underneath,*
*A pint-pot neatly graven.*

The 'Daydream' gives a very good illustration of the change in Tennyson's attitude since 1830. In his volume of that year he included, under the title 'The Sleeping Beauty', four romantic stanzas describing the Princess on her couch, deep in the magic sleep which cannot be broken except by the advent of the Fairy Prince. In 1842 he added to this a charming and fanciful 'Prologue', 'Moral', 'Envoi' and 'Epilogue', addressed to an imaginary Lady Flora, whose heart the Poet is seeking to win by his fable; a description of the sleeping Palace, with a pendant ('The Revival') depicting the sudden awakening of the King and his Court when the charm is snapped; and a beautiful love scene as the Princess and Prince go off together to seek his father's Court. These are the four stanzas of 'The Revival':

*A touch, a kiss! the charm was snapt,*
*There rose a noise of striking clocks,*
*And feet that ran, and doors that clapt,*
*And barking dogs, and crowing cocks;*
*A fuller light illumined all,*
*A breeze through all the garden swept,*
*A sudden hubbub shook the hall,*
*And sixty feet the fountain leapt.*

*The hedge broke in, the banner blew,*
*The butler drank, the steward scrawl'd,*
*The fire shot up, the martin flew,*
*The parrot scream'd, the peacock squall'd,*
*The maid and page renew'd their strife,*
*The palace bang'd, and buzz'd and clackt,*
*And all the long-pent stream of life*
*Dash'd downward in a cataract.*

*And last with these the king awoke,*
*And in his chair himself uprear'd,*
*And yawn'd, and rubb'd his face, and spoke,*
*'By holy rood, a royal beard!*
*How say you? we have slept, my lords,*
*My beard has gown into my lap.'*
*The barons swore, with many words,*
*'Twas but an after-dinner's nap.*

*'Pardy,' return'd the king, 'but still*
*My joints are somewhat stiff or so.*
*My lord, and shall we pass the bill*
*I mention'd half an hour ago?'*
*The chancellor, sedate and vain,*
*In courteous words return'd reply:*
*But dallied with his golden chain,*
*And, smiling, put the question by.*

In 'The Talking Oak', Olivia's lover finds a huge old oak tree in her father's park miraculously endowed with a voice, and the two discourse of her charms and of her superiority to the maidens of earlier days who have sheltered beneath the tree's spreading branches, and whose fashions and follies are delightfully hit off. The stanzas in which the oak describes his last vision of Olivia may serve as a specimen of the whole:

*'O yesterday, you know, the fair*
*Was holden at the town;*
*Her father left his good arm-chair,*
*And rode his hunter down.*

*'And with him Albert came on his.*
*I look'd at him with joy:*
*As cowslip unto oxslip is,*
*So seems she to the boy.*

*'An hour had past—and, sitting straight*
*Within the low-wheel'd chaise,*
*Her mother trundled to the gate*
*Behind the dappled grays.*

*'But as for her, she stay'd at home,*
*And on the roof she went,*
*And down the way you use to come,*
*She look'd with discontent.*

*'She left the novel half-uncut*
*Upon the rosewood shelf;*
*She left the new piano shut:*
*She could not please herself.*

*'Then ran she, gamesome as the colt,*
*And livelier than a lark*
*She sent her voice tnro' all the holt*
*Before her, and the park.*

*'A light wind chased her on the wing,*
*And in the chase grew wild,*
*As close as might be would he cling*
*About the darling child:*

*'But light as any wind that blows*
*So fleetly did she stir,*
*The flower, she touch'd on, dipt and rose*
*And turn'd to look at her.'*

In another poem in the same vein the Poet uses the old legend of Amphion, who could make the trees dance at his bidding, to illustrate the difference between the conditions under which a nineteenth-century poet had to work and those of the first great ages of classic art. The poem has humour and charm, but is not so successful as those already mentioned, nor is 'The Goose', a humorous ballad which is said to have been intended as a political allegory, though I have never been able to discover its exact significance.

All these poems in the 1842 volume were written during the late 1830s, some of the most miserable years in the Poet's life. The early 1840s were made equally bitter to him, first by the breaking off, under her family's pressure, of his engagement to Emily Sellwood, and then by the loss, at the end of 1842, of the whole of his small capital in an imprudent speculation.

These reverses had for some time a serious effect on his health. The grant of a pension from the Civil List in 1845 improved his financial position and helped to restore his mental and physical state. It also gave him occasion for one of his rare experiments in satire, a form of expression which he usually found distasteful.[1] Bulwer Lytton, who was a leader of the school of critics most hostile to Tennyson, and had been trying to secure a pension for a protégé of his own, and was extremely incensed at the grant, and inserted in a poem he was publishing anonymously in instalments, under the title of *The New Timon*, a violent and most unfair attack on Tennyson's poetry, with a very misleading reference to his financial position. Tennyson in reply composed some lines,

[1] It was perhaps for this reason that he never published the following sonnet (probably written in 1836), which appeared for the first time in the *Unpublished Early Poems* of 1931.

*Sonnet*

*How thought you that this thing could captivate?*
*What are those graces that could make her dear,*
*Who is not worth the notice of a sneer*
*To rouse the vapid devil of her hate?*
*A speech conventional, so void of weight*
*That after it has buzzed about one's ear,*
*'Twere rich refreshment for a week to hear*
*The dentist babble or the barber prate;*
*A hand displayed with many a little art;*
*An eye that glances on her neighbour's dress;*
*A foot too often shown for my regard;*
*An angel's form—a waiting-woman's heart;*
*A perfect-featured face, expressionless,*
*Insipid as the Queen upon a card.*

making fun of Lytton's literary pretensions and notorious dandyism, which he sent to his friend, John Forster, without any instruction as to what should be done with them. Forster was very much annoyed with Lytton for steadily refusing to admit his authorship of *The New Timon*, and sent the verses to *Punch*, where they duly appeared under the title *The New Timon and the Poets* over the signature 'Alcibiades'.

The following extract will show that had Tennyson wished he could have become a most effective satirist:

*We knew him out of Shakespeare's art,*
*And those fine curses which he spoke;*
*The old Timon, with his noble heart,*
*That, strongly loathing, greatly broke.*

*So died the Old: here comes the New:*
*Regard him: a familiar face.*
*I* thought *we knew him: What, it's you*
*The padded man—that wears the stays—*

*Who killed the girls and thrill'd the boys*
*With dandy pathos when you wrote,*
*A Lion, you, that made a noise,*
*And shook a mane* en papillotes.

. . . . .

You *talk of tinsel! Why, we see*
*The old mark of rouge upon your cheeks.*
You *prate of nature! you are he*
*That spilt his life about the cliques.*

*A Timon you! Nay, nay, for shame:*
*It looks too arrogant a jest—*
*The fierce old man—to take* his *name,*
*You bandbox. Off, and let him rest.*

Tennyson now felt able to set about the completion of the most important humorous poem he was ever to attempt, that extraordinary blend of burlesque, passion and philosophy, *The*

*Princess*. I call *The Princess* a humorous poem in spite of the high level of much of its thought and emotion, for the original scheme (involving the foundation by an idealistic and headstrong girl of a woman's University, from which all men were to be rigidly excluded) was undoubtedly conceived in the spirit of comedy. This does not mean that Tennyson thought the subject of woman's rights and social position one of small importance. Had he done so he would never have devoted to it, almost at the peak of his powers, a poem of over 3000 lines. But he realized that the controversy had aroused hysterical enthusiasm on one side and a great deal of prejudice and ridicule on the other, and he wished his statement of the issues to be one that would attract, without inflaming the passions of the contending parties. As the poem progressed, however, the importance of his theme affected him more and more, and the element of comedy gradually dwindled, disappearing altogether from the last two cantos.

It is difficult to give by quotation any adequate idea of so long and complex a poem. Its basic theme is admirably comic, involving the contrast between the Princess's aims and the hopeless absurdity of her scheme, founded on a deliberate ignoring of the greatest fundamental fact of human nature. Indeed, the Princess, the finest of all Tennyson's female characters, has every virtue except that sense of humour which the Poet himself valued so highly. Excellently comic, too, is the situation of the Prince and his two friends disguised as girls amongst the undergraduates of the woman's University—when, for example, after spending the morning in attendance at the lectures of the various female professors, they issue, 'gorged with knowledge'—

> *. . . like three horses that have broken fence*
> *And glutted all night long breast deep in corn*

and the Prince exclaims:

> '*Why, Sirs, they do all this as well as we!*'

There is much admirable comedy of character. Particularly effective in contrast with the high-souled, iron-willed visionary Princess Ida, are her small, fussy, good-natured, ineffective father King Gama, and her huge, brainless, devoted brother Arac.

Admirable is the speech in which the King explains to the Princess's suitor that she has repudiated her engagement to him.

*His name was Gama; crack'd and small his voice,*
*But bland the smile that like a wrinkling wind*
*On glassy water drove his cheek in lines;*
*A little dry old man, without a star,*
*Not like a king: three days he feasted us,*
*And on the fourth I spake of why we came,*
*And my betroth'd. 'You do us, Prince,' he said,*
*Airing a snowy hand and signet gem,*
*'All honour. We remember love ourselves*
*In our sweet youth: there did a compact pass*
*Long summers back, a kind of ceremony—*
*I think the year in which our olives fail'd.*
*I would you had her, Prince, with all my heart,*
*With my full heart: but there were widows here,*
*Two widows, Lady Psyche, Lady Blanche;*
*They fed her theories, in and out of place*
*Maintaining that with equal husbandry*
*The woman were an equal to the man.*
*They harp'd on this; with this our banquets rang;*
*Our dances broke and buzz'd in knots of talk;*
*Nothing but this; my very ears were hot*
*To hear them: knowledge, so my daughter held,*
*Was all in all: they had but been, she thought,*
*As children; they must lose the child, assume*
*The woman: then, Sir, awful odes she wrote,*
*Too awful, sure, for what they treated of,*
*But all she is and does is awful; odes*
*About this losing of the child; and rhymes*
*And dismal lyrics, prophesying change*
*Beyond all reason: these the women sang;*
*And they that know such things—I sought but peace;*
*No critic I—would call them masterpieces:*
*They master'd* me. *At last she begg'd a boon,*
*A certain summer-palace which I have*
*Hard by your father's frontier: I said no,*
*Yet being an easy man, gave it: and there,*

*All wild to found an University*
*For maidens, on the spur she fled; and more*
*We know not,—only this: they see no men,*
*Not ev'n her brother Arac, nor the twins*
*Her brethren, tho' they love her, look upon her*
*As on a kind of paragon; and I*
*(Pardon me saying it) were much loth to breed*
*Dispute betwixt myself and mine: but since*
*(And I confess with right) you think me bound*
*In some sort, I can give you letters to her:*
*And yet, to speak the truth, I rate your chance*
*Almost at naked nothing.'*

Arac's character comes out in his defence of his sister to the Prince:

*'She flies too high, she flies too high! and yet*
*She ask'd but space and fairplay for her scheme;*
*She prest and prest it on me—I myself,*
*What know I of these things? but, life and soul!*
*I thought her half-right talking of her wrongs;*
*I say she flies too high, 'sdeath! what of that?*
*I take her for the flower of womankind,*
*And so I often told her, right or wrong,*
*And Prince, she can be sweet to those she loves,*
*And, right or wrong, I care not: this is all,*
*I stand upon her side: she made me swear it—*
*'Sdeath—and with solemn rites by candlelight—*
*Swear by St. something—I forget her name—*
*Her that talk'd down the fifty wisest men;*
She *was a princess too; and so I swore.*
*Come, this is all; she will not: waive your claim'*:

From these few quotations it will be seen that *The Princess* contains some excellent comic writing and that much of it breathes the true spirit of comedy. In spite of the high emotional tension of the later cantos, and the solemnity of its close, it remains a true comedy in the mediaeval sense. Tennyson added to it, as he had done to the 'Morte d'Arthur', a Prologue and Epilogue in his *English Idyl* vein. The scene of these is set at a picnic in a Kentish park, where the meal is laid out in the ruins of a mediaeval Abbey, while down below the Village Institute is holding a fête, with sports and dancing and, for side-shows, such essentially modern contrivances as fire balloons, parachutes and electrical and mechanical toys and models. Out of the talk at this picnic the story of the Princess's University arises, and is told in chapters by a party of young Cambridge men, partly to tease the lady members of the party. The Prologue and Epilogue are carried out with great finesse and charm, leading the reader's mind very cleverly up to the strangely conceived and constructed poem, and firmly and pleasantly establishing its comedy atmosphere and serious overtones.

For the next twenty-five years Tennyson's energies were mainly occupied with works which, in his conception of them, did not admit much scope for humour: *In Memoriam* (1850) (most of which had, however, been written before *The Princess*), *Maud* (1855) and the *Idylls of the King* (1859, 1869 and 1872). The succeeding ten years he spent mainly on dramatic work, chiefly in the domain of tragedy, where he considered that only a certain formal humour was possible under the prevailing conditions of the stage, and that even this must be kept in strict subservience to the plot.

Although humour had undoubtedly played a large part in Tennyson's friendship with Arthur Hallam, the intense feeling that permeates *In Memoriam* and the lofty tone of its speculations would have made any suspicion of humorous treatment incongruous. The hero of *Maud*, like the Princess and the hero of 'Locksley Hall' and 'Sixty Years After', obviously had no sense of humour. He was what Tennyson himself might have been in his youth, had he lacked that saving quality. A considerable gift of satire he had, and this comes out in the descriptions of Maud's brother:

*the oil'd and curl'd Assyrian bull*

who 'gorgonizes' the lover 'from head to foot with a stony British stare', and of Maud's rival suitor, the weak-minded son of a recently ennobled coal magnate:

*A lord, a captain, a padded shape,*
*A bought Commission, a waxen face,*
*A rabbit mouth that is ever agape—*

In earlier unpublished versions the satire is even sharper, for the passage continued:

> *Captain? he to hold a command!*
> *He can hold a cue, he can pocket a ball.*
> *And, sure, not a bantam cockerel lives*
> *With a weaker crow upon English land,*
> *Whether he boasts of a horse that gains,*
> *Or cackles his own applause, when he gives*
> *A filthy story at second-hand,*
> *Where the point is miss'd, and the filth remains.*

Nor did Tennyson's conception of the *Idylls of the King* give much scope for humour, and he wisely made no attempt to re-create Malory's tedious buffoon, Sir Dinadan. Almost the only exception is his introduction in 'The Last Tournament' of King Arthur's fool Dagonet, whose satirical exchange of witticisms with Sir Tristram emphasizes the decadence and presages the ruin of the Round Table. But Dagonet must have been rather a melancholy jester at his brightest.

> . . . *'I have wallow'd, I have wash'd—the world*
> *Is flesh and shadow—I have had my day.*
> *The dirty nurse, Experience, in her kind*
> *Has foul'd me—an' I wallow'd then I wash'd.*
> *I have had my day and my philosophies—*
> *And thank the Lord I am King Arthur's fool.'*

However, in the 'Enoch Arden' volume, issued in 1864 when work on the *Idylls* was temporarily at a standstill, Tennyson published the first of a series of poems in the Lincolnshire dialect which were to be his last and most characteristic contribution to the literature of humour. These poems, which are all monologues by characters such as he had known in his childhood and youth in and about Somersby, were startlingly different from anything that he had published before. The use of the broad Lincolnshire dialect (a trace of which marked his own speech throughout his life) seemed to free him from the inhibitions imposed on him by his fastidious taste when he was using the literary English which he had developed to a new refinement. The crude, rich, earthy language of the peasants, craftsmen and farmers, whom he had known so intimately, their hard, narrow natures, their toughness and self-sufficiency, came to life again under his touch with results which can challenge comparison with the best work in the same field of Scott and Burns.

The first of these poems, 'Northern Farmer'—*Old Style*—is spoken by a tough, earthy old farmer who lies dying. He rails at the nurse for refusing to bring him his night-cap pint of ale, and at the doctor for forbidding it. The parson has been reminding him that his tithes are unpaid and talking of his sins, particularly his slip with Bessy Morris years ago; but he pays up the tithe and can say that he had maintained the bastard, so what is there to complain of? The real thing that bothers him is his land and the 800 acres he farms for the Squire. The Almighty's intervention is no more reasonable than that of the nurse or the doctor.[1]

*Do godamighty knaw what e's doing a-taäkin' o' meä?*
*I beänt wonn as saws 'ere a beän an' yonder a peä;*
*An' Squire 'ull be sa mad an' all—a' dear a' dear!*
*And I 'a managed for Squire coom Michaelmas thutty year.*

*'E mowt 'a taäen owd Joänes, as 'ant not a 'aäporth o' sense,*
*Or 'e mowt 'a taäen young Robins—'e niver mended a fence:*
*But godamighty 'e moost taäke meä and' taäke ma now*
*Wi' 'aäf the cows to cauve an' Thurnaby hoälms to plow!*

. . . . .

*Squire's i' Lunnon, an' summun I reckons 'ull 'ave to write,*
*For whoä's to howd the land ater meä that muddles me quite;*
*Sartin-sewer I beä, that e weänt niver give it to Joänes,*
*Naw, nor 'e moänt to Robins—'e niver rembles the stoäns.*

*But summun 'ull come ater meä mayhap wi' 'is kittle o' steäm*
*Huzzin' and' maäzin' the blessed feälds wi' the Divil's oän teäm.*
*Sin' I mun die I mun die, thaw life they says is sweet,*
*But sin' I mun die I mun die, for I couldn't abeär to see it.*

*What atta stannin' theer fur, an' doesn' bring ma the aäle?*
*Doctor's a 'toättler, lass, an' 'e's hallus i' the owd taäle;*
*I weänt break rules for Doctor, 'e knows naw moor nor a fly;*
*Git me ma aäle, I tell tha, an' if I mun die I mun die.*

[1] To appreciate these poems fully one should imagine them being read aloud in a style of broad comedy, *e.g.*, by Mr. Stanley Holloway.

This poem was followed in 1869 by 'Northern Farmer'—*New Style*—a strong contrast. For the old tough sense of duty is substituted an unashamed self-seeking. The farmer is chiding his son for wanting to marry the penniless parson's daughter. He has a savage contempt for poverty.

*'Tis'n them as 'as munny as breäks into 'ouses an' steäls,*
*Them as 'as coats to their backs an' taäkes their regular meäls.*
*Noä, but it's them as niver knaws wheer a meäl's to be 'ad.*
*Taäke my word for it, Sammy, the poor in a loomp is bad. . . .*

He is determined that the boy shall 'marry a good 'un' or he will leave the farm to his younger son.

*Do'ant be stunt;*[1] *taäke time: I knaws what maäkes tha sa mad.*
*Warn't I craäzed fur the lasses mysén when I wur a lad?*
*But I knaw'd a Quaäker feller as often 'as towd me this:*
*'Doänt thou marry for munny, but goä wheer munny is!'*

*An' I went wheer munny war: an' thy muther coom to 'and,*
*Wi' lots o' munny laäid by, an' a nicetish bit o' land.*
*Maäybe she warn't a beauty:—I niver giv it a thowt—*
*But warn't she as good to cuddle an' kiss as a lass as 'ant nowt?*

. . . . .

*Luvv? what's luvv? thou can luvv thy lass an' 'er munny too,*
*Maäkin' 'em goä togither as they've good right to do.*
*Could'n I luvv thy muther by cause o' 'er munny laäid by?*
*Naäy—fur I luvv'd 'er a vast sight moor fur it: reäson why.*

*Ay an' thy muther says thou wants to marry the lass,*
*Cooms of a gentleman born: an' we boäth on us thinks tha an ass.*

Eleven years (spent mainly in dramatic work) passed before Tennyson published (in 1880) another collection of lyrics and ballads. This included two more dialect poems. In the first which I shall quote, 'The Village Wife', the sex of the speaker is changed, but the analysis is still unsparingly objective. This time it is the village gossip, who describes with pitiless gusto the decline and fall of the late Squire and his family—a theme which could easily fill a novel of 100,000 words. In about 160 lines the narrator not

[1] Obstinate.

only makes it alive with what seems a volume of significant detail, but at the same time lavishly exposes her own callousness, ignorance and conceit. A good specimen of her chatter is the following description of the foolish, good-natured Squire, who squanders his estate in the futile activities of a would-be connoisseur:

*An' Squire wur hallus a-smilin', an' gied to the tramps goin' by—*
*An' all o' the wust i' the parish—wi' hoffens a drop in 'is eye.*
*An' ivry darter o' Squire's hed her awn ridin-'orse to 'ersen,*
*An' they rampaged about wi' their grooms, an' was 'untin' arter the men,*
*An' hallus a-dallackt*[1] *an' dizen'd out, an' a-buyin' new cloäthes,*
*While 'e sit like a great glimmer-gowk*[2] *wi' 'is glasses athurt 'is noäse,*
*An' 'is noäse sa grufted wi' snuff es it couldn't be scroob'd awaäy,*
*Fur atween 'is readin' an' writin' 'e snift up a box in a daäy,*
*An' 'e niver runn'd arter the fox, nor arter the birds wi' 'is gun,*
*An' 'e niver not shot one 'are, but 'e leäved it to Charlie 'is son,*
*An' 'e niver not fish'd 'is awn ponds, but Charlie 'e cotch'd the pike,*
*For 'e warn't not born to the land, an' 'e didn't take kind to it like;*
*But I ears es 'e'd gie fur a howry*[3] *owd book thutty pound an' moor,*
*An' 'e'd wrote an owd book, his awn sen, so I knaw'd es'e'd coom to be poor;*
*An' 'e gied—I be fear'd fur to tell tha 'ow much—fur an owd scratted stoän,*
*An' 'e digg'd up a loomp i' the land an' 'e got a brown pot an' a boän,*
*An' 'e bowt owd money, es wouldn't goä, wi' good gowd o' the Queen,*
*An 'e bowt little statutes all-naäkt an' which was a shaäme to be seen;*
*But 'e niver loookt ower a bill, nor 'e niver not seed to owt,*
*An' 'e niver knawd nowt but booöks, an' booöks, as thou knows, beänt nowt.*

and the following is the gossip's account of the break-up of the family after the death of the only son through a riding accident:

*So 'is taäil*[4] *wur lost an' 'is booöks wur gone an' 'is boy wur dead,*
*An' Squire 'e smiled an' 'e smiled, but 'e niver not lift oop 'is 'ead;*
*Hallus a soft un Squire! an' 'e smiled, fur 'e hedn't naw friend,*
*Sa feyther an' son was buried together, an' this wur the hend.*

[1] Overdrest in gay colours. [2] Owl. [3] Filthy.

[4] The entailed estate would pass out of the Squire's family owing to the death of his only son.

*An' Parson as hesn't the call, nor the mooney, but hes the pride,*
*'E reäds of a sewer an' sartan 'oäp o' the tother side;*
*But I beänt that sewer es the Lord, howsiver they praäy'd an' praäy'd,*
*Let's them inter 'eaven eäsy es leäves their debts to be paäid.*
*'Siver*[1] *the mou'ds rattled down upo' poor owd Squire i' the wood,*[2]
*An' I cried along wi' the gells, fur they weänt niver coom to naw good.*

*Fur Molly the long un she walkt awaäy wi' a hofficer lad,*
*An' nawbody 'eard on 'er sin, so o' coorse she be gone to the bad!*
*An' Lucy wur laäme o' one leg, sweet'arts she niver 'ed none—*
*Straänge an' unheppen*[3] *Miss Lucy! we naämed her 'Dot an' gaw one!'*
*An' Hetty wur weäk i' the hattics, wi'out ony harm i' the legs,*
*An' the fever'ed baäked Jinny's 'ead as bald as one o' them heggs,*
*An' Nelly wur up fro' the craädle as big i' the mouth as a cow,*
*An' saw she mun hammergrate,*[4] *lass, or she weänt git a maäte onyhow!*
*An' es for Miss Annie es call'd me afoor my awn foälks to my faäce*
*'A hignorant village wife as 'ud hev to be larn'd her own plaäce,'*
*Hes fur Miss Hannie the heldest as now be a-grawin' sa howd,*
*I knaws that mooch o' sheä, es it beänt not fit to be towd!*

*Sa I didn't not taäke it kindly of owd Miss Annie to saäy*
*Es I should be talkin ageän 'em, es soon es they went awaäy,*
*Fur, lawks! 'ow I cried when they went, an' our Nelly she gied me 'er 'and,*
*Fur I'd ha done owt for the Squire an' 'is gells es belong'd to the land;*
*Booöks, es I said afoor, thebbe neyther 'ere nor theer!*
*But I sarved 'em wi' butter an' heggs fur huppuds o' twenty year.*

After this, the dialect poems become more genial in their outlook. In 'The Northern Cobbler' the toughness, candour and self-sufficiency of the race are turned to good account in the cobbler's description of his fight to free himself from the drink habit, which gets hold of him when his faithful Sally has her first baby. Things go from bad to worse, and at last even she turns against him and becomes 'a tongue-banger'.[5]

[1] However. [2] Coffin. [3] Ungainly, awkward.
[4] Emigrate. [5] Scold.

*. . . . 'Sottin' thy braäins*
*Guzzlin' an' soäkin' an' smoäkin' an hawmin'*[1] *about i' the laänes,*
*Soä sow-droonk that tha doesn' not touch thy 'at to the Squire';*
*An' I looök'd cock-eyed at my noäse an' I seeäd 'im a-gittin' o' fire;*
*But sin' I wur hallus i' liquor an' hallus as droonk as a king,*
*Foälks' coostom flitted awaäy like a kite wi' a brokken string.*

*An' one night I cooms 'oäm like a bull gotten loose at a faäir,*
*An' she wur a-waäitin' for me, an' cryin' and tearin' 'er 'aäir,*
*An' I tummled athurt the crädle an' sweär'd as I'd break ivry stick*
*O' furnitur 'ere 'i the 'ouse, an' I gied our Sally a kick,*
*An' I mash'd the taäbles an' chairs, an' she an' the babby beäl'd,*[2]
*Fur I knaw'd naw moor what I did nor a mortal beäst o' the feäld.*

After this he promises amendment, and is ultimately able to boast his success:

*So like a greät num-cumpus I blubber'd awaäy o' the bed—*
*'Weänt niver do it naw moor'; an' Sally looökt up an' she said,*
*'I'll upowd it*[3] *tha weänt; thou'rt like the rest o' the men,*
*Thou'll goä sniffin' about the tap till tha does it ageän.*
*Theer's thy hennemy, man, an' I knaws, as knaws tha sa well,*
*That, if tha seeäs 'im an' smells 'im tha'll foller 'im slick into Hell.'*

*'Naäy,' says I, 'fur I weänt goä sniffin' about the tap.'*
*'Weänt tha?' she says, an' mysen I thowt i' mysen 'mayhap.'*
*'Noä': an' I started awaäy like a shot, an' down to the Hinn,*
*An' I browt what tha seeäs stannin' theer, yon big black bottle o' gin.*

*'That caps owt,'*[4] *says Sally, an' saw she begins to cry.*
*But I puts it inter 'er 'ands an' I says to 'er, 'Sally,' says I,*
*'Stan' 'im theer i' the naäme o' the Lord an' the power ov 'is Graäce,*
*Stan' 'im theer, fur I'll looök my hennemy strait i' the faäce.*
*Stan' 'im theer i' the winder, an' let ma looök at 'im then,*
*'E seeäms naw moor nor watter, an' 'e's the Divil's oän sen.'*

[1] Lounging.
[2] Bellowed, cried out.
[3] I'll uphold it.
[4] That's beyond everything.

*An' I wur down i' the mouth, couldn't do naw work an' all,*
*Nasty an' snaggy an' shaäky, an' poonch'd my 'and wi' the hawl,*
*But she wur a power o' coomfut, an' settled 'ersen o' my knee,*
*An' coaxd an' coodled me oop till ageän I feel'd mysen free.*

*An' Sally she tell'd it about, an' foälk stood a-gawmin'*[1] *in,*
*As thaw it wur summat bewitch'd istead of a quart o' gin;*
*An' some of 'em said it wur watter—an' I wur chousin' the wife,*
*Fur I couldn't 'owd 'ands off gin, wur it nobbut to saäve my life;*
*An' blacksmith 'e strips me the thick ov 'is airm, an' 'e shaws it to me,*
*'Feëal thou this! thou can't graw this upo' watter!' says he.*
*An' Doctor 'e calls o' Sunday an' just as candles was lit,*
*'Thou moänt do it,' he says, 'tha mun breäk 'im off bit by bit.'*
*'Thou'rt but a Methody-man,' says Parson, and laäys down 'is 'at,*
*An' 'e points to the bottle o' gin, 'but I respecks tha fur that';*
*An' Squire, his oän very sen, walks down fro' the 'All to see,*
*An' 'e spanks 'is 'and into mine, 'fur I respecks tha,' says 'e;*
*An' coostom ageän draw'd in like a wind fro' far an' wide,*
*And browt me the booöts to be cobbled fro' hafe the coontry-side.*

*An' theer 'e stans an' theer 'e shall stan to my dying daäy;*
*I 'a gotten to loov 'im ageän in another kind of a waäy,*
*Proud on 'im, like, my lad, an' I keeäps 'im cleän an' bright,*
*Loovs 'im, an' roobs 'im, an' doosts 'im, an' puts 'im back i' the light.*

*An' once I said to the Missis, 'My lass, when I cooms to die,*
*Smash the bottle to smithers, the Divil's in 'im,' said I.*
*But arter I chaänged my mind, an' if Sally be left aloän,*
*I'll hev 'im a-buried wi'mma an taäke 'im afoor the Throän.*

In the next poem of the series, 'The Spinster's Sweet-Arts', the speaker is again a woman, but this time the treatment is entirely genial. In it the Old Maid, who has doggedly avoided matrimony in order not to lose control of her two hundred a year, explains to her tom-cats, whom she has named after her various suitors, the advantage of spinsterhood and her reasons for rejecting them. This is a piece of pure high spirits delightfully carried out, but lacking the solidity of the earlier poems. I will quote two passages: the first giving the spinster's idea of children:

[1] Staring vacantly.

*But I niver not wished fer childer, I hev'nt naw liking fer brats;*
*Pretty anew when ya dresses 'em oop, an' they gaws fer a walk,*
*Or sits with their 'ands afoor 'em, and doesn't not 'inder the talk!*
*But their bottles o' pap, an' their mucky bibs, and the clats an' the clouts,*
*An' their mashin' their toys to pieäces an' maäkin' ma deaf wi' their shouts,*
*An' hallus a-joompin' about ma as if they was set upo' springs,*
*An' a haxin' ma hawkward questions, an' saäyin' ondecent things,*
*An' a-callin' ma 'hugly' mayhap to my faäce an' tearin' my gown. . . .*

The second passage is equally uncomplimentary to man in the home:

*To be horder'd about, an waäked, when Molly'd put out the light,*
*By a man coomin' in wi' a hiccup at ony hour o' the night!*
*An' the taäble staäined wi' 'is aäle, an' the mud of his boots o' the stairs,*
*An' the stink o' 'is pipe i' the 'ouse, an' the mark o' 'is 'ead o' the chairs!*
*An' noän o' my four sweet-arts 'ud 'a let me 'a hed my oän waäy,*
*Sa I likes 'em best wi' taäils when they 'evnt a word to saäy.*

After this in 1889 came 'Owd Roa', the story of the old dog (Rover) who has saved the farmer's child from death when his farm was burned to the ground. This is a brilliantly objective description by the farmer of the Christmas Eve, when the fire surprises him asleep in his kitchen, and of the fire's disastrous progress; while, as in the earlier poems, the narrator, by a few perfectly natural and hardly perceptible touches, makes his own character and that of his wife come out just as clearly as the rush and roar of the flames and the crash of the bricks and timber when the roof gives way.

So strong a hold on the Poet's imagination had these memories of old Lincolnshire days and ways that, within a few months of his death, when almost eighty-three years old, he created one more poem for the series, which appeared as 'The Churchwarden and the Curate' in his posthumous volume, *The Death of Oenone and other Poems*. This, again, was in the Poet's more genial mood. In it the Churchwarden of Owlby-cum-Scratby advises the Vicar's son, who has just been ordained, what to do if he wishes to get on in the Church—a profession of which the old man takes a very materialistic view, cheerfully lacking in respect for the priestly office:

*Well—sin ther beä chuch-wardens (he says), ther' mun be parsons an' all,*
*An' if t'one stick alongside t'uther the chuch wëant happen a fall.*

Rather unconvincingly he attributes his own remarkable success in life to a policy of deliberate self-repression.

*For if ever thy fether had riled me I kep' mysen meeäk as a lamb,*
*And saw by the Graäce of the Lord, Mr. Harry, I ham what I ham.*

This policy he forcibly recommends to his young protégé: contrasting his own prudence with the vicar's unworldly frankness:

*But Parson 'e* will *speäk out, saw, now 'e be sixty-seven,*
*He'll niver swap Owlby an' Scratby for owt but the Kingdom o' Heaven;*
*An' thou'll be 'is Curate 'ere, but, if iver tha meäns to git 'igher,*
*Tha mun tackle the sins o' the World, an' not the faults o' the Squire.*
*An' I reckons tha'll light of a livin' somewhere i' the Wowd*[1] *or the Fen,*
*If tha cottons down to thy betters, an' keeäps thysen to thysen.*
*But niver not speäk plaaïn out, if tha wants to git forrards a bit,*
*But creeäp along the hedge-bottoms, an' thou'll be a Bishop yet.*

The only sign of weakening in this poem by the eighty-three-year-old humorist is the intrusion of a rather heavy-handed joke about the Baptists 'weshing' themselves in the Churchwarden's pond and poisoning his cow.

When one surveys Tennyson's work from *The Devil and the Lady* to 'The Churchwarden and the Curate', it is evident that he possessed true comic genius, but that his deeply serious and emotional temperament, and his intense spiritual suffering during the years of adolescence and early manhood, did not for some time allow him to give this full and direct expression. Even in the boyish play, which was clearly planned as an entirely comic work, seriousness 'kept breaking in'; and *The Princess*, which began as pure comedy, moved—to use Tennyson's own words in the Epilogue—'in a strange diagonal', and came at the end 'to quite a solemn close'. As he emerged into maturity, his increasing detachment and objectivity enabled him to evolve two types of

[1] 'Wowd', wold.

poem through which he could give his sense of humour refined and subtle expression—the *English Idyls* and the 'Horatian' poems. After the publication of *The Princess*, he devoted his main energies, for over thirty years, to very different types of work—*In Memoriam*, the intense and hectic love poem *Maud*, the *Idylls of the King* and the poetic drama. But during these years he found time and energy to develop an entirely new type of dialect poem, based on his recollection of his childhood and youth in Lincolnshire, which, more than anything else that he wrote, express the rustic strength, sledge-hammer common sense and sardonic humour which his friends knew well as facets of his many sided nature.

This substantial volume of directly humorous work, added to Tennyson's occasional experiments with satire and the macabre, show a humorous talent of power and variety which cannot be matched by any of our poets since Shakespeare, but which both the critics of his own day and those of the present century have strangely neglected.

II

# *Tennyson's Politics*

IT WAS INEVITABLE that Tennyson, with his universality of mind, which so impressed FitzGerald, and his intense patriotism should, from his youth onwards, take a continuous and vital interest in Britain's domestic and foreign politics. But as he was, before everything, a creative artist, his interest was likely to be instinctive, not giving allegiance to any single political creed or party, and reflected in his poetry not so much by direct references to current events—though these are by no means entirely absent—as in his reaction to the political theories and tendencies which from time to time excited his admiration or opposition.

He was brought up under the shadow of the French Revolution and the Napoleonic wars, for he was nearly six years old when the Battle of Waterloo was fought in June 1815, and remembered all his life seeing the stage coach drive by, the horses and whips decorated with white ribbons in honour of the great victory. The Tennyson family were Whigs by tradition, and Charles, the Poet's uncle (who afterwards inherited the family estate of Bayons Manor and changed his name to d'Eyncourt), became a member of Parliament for Grimsby in 1818 and soon joined the extreme left wing of the Party. Although the relations between Somersby and Bayons were far from friendly, the boy shared his uncle's political views, as some of his contributions to *Poems by Two Brothers* (published in 1827) show, for example, his poems of encouragement addressed to the Greeks in their struggle against their Turkish masters and to the revolutionaries who were attacking the Monarchy in Spain.

At the end of 1827 Tennyson went up to Cambridge and there soon became one of a set of young men with strongly Liberal views. Frederick Denison Maurice, who later became the founder of the Christian Socialist movement, had been one of the leaders of this set, which in 1829 became actively associated with a plan to help some refugees in England to revive the Spanish revolutionary movement. In 1830 Tennyson and his friend, Arthur Hallam, went together to the Pyrenees to carry money and despatches to the Confederate Party there. They were both disgusted by the selfishness and corruption of the Spanish revolutionaries, whose movement was easily suppressed, one of the young Englishmen involved in it suffering summary execution. This experience probably did something to check Tennyson's revolutionary ardour, which received a further check when he and Hallam returned to England. The movement for the Reform of the Franchise had been gathering strength throughout the 1820s, Charles Tennyson being one of its leaders in Parliament and Alfred and his friends enthusiastic supporters. The autumn and winter of 1830 were marked by violent Reform agitations all over the country. In Cambridgeshire and elsewhere there were outbursts of rick burning, and Tennyson spent some exciting hours up to his knees in mud and water passing buckets from well to blazing rickyard, while the air re-echoed the shrieks of scorching animals and the cattle galloped in clumsy panic about the fields. There were rumours that the rioters meant to attack the town, and Tennyson and his friends paraded, armed with stout clubs, for its defence. A ballad, afterwards published by his friends Henry and Frank Lushington, gives an amusing picture of Tennyson's reaction to these events:

*Unto the poet wise we spoke*
*'Is any law of battle broke*
*By pouring from afar*
*Water or oil or molten lead?'*
*The Poet raised his massive head—*
*'Confound the laws of war!'*

These experiences gave him a strong distaste for revolutionary methods, and in two sonnets, written apparently about 1832 but not published until a hundred years later (see *Unpublished Early Poems*, pp. 61 and 62), he protested against the 'Sophisters' of party politics and the 'mob rhetoric' of the 'Lords of the hustings', which he feared might shatter England's 'solid peace', rather oddly classing together as 'brass-mouthed demagogues' Daniel O'Connell and Joseph Hume, an unfavourable view which, in

O'Connell's case at least, he later came to revise. But these reactions did not damp his enthusiasm for the Cause itself, and when the Bill passed the House of Lords in the following year he and his sisters celebrated the event by ringing the church bells at Somersby, to the great annoyance of the Conservative Rector.

The volumes published in 1830 and 1832 gave no indication of the keen interest which Tennyson had taken in these political movements, except for one good Miltonic sonnet on the Polish insurrection of 1830. Then in the autumn of 1833 Arthur Hallam died, and Tennyson entered into the nine years' silence that was not to be broken until the appearance of his two famous volumes of 1842. But he had, during 1833, expressed the convictions which the political experiences of the preceding years had given him, in three poems:

> *You ask me why though ill at ease . . .*
> *Of old sat Freedom on the heights . . . and*
> *Love thou thy land. . . .*

In these poems (ultimately published in the second of the volumes of 1842) he endeavoured to state his own political creed in a series of compressed and not always easily interpreted aphorisms. In the first he expressed in lines that have become proverbial, his passionate love of England:

> *. . . the land that freemen till,*
> *That sober-suited Freedom chose,*
> *The land, where girt with friends or foes*
> *A man may speak the thing he will:*
>
> *A land of settled government,*
> *A land of just and old renown,*
> *Where Freedom slowly broadens down*
> *From precedent to precedent.*

In freedom of thought and speech he saw the only hope of truth, justice and law. Truth could not be evolved unless

> *Set in all lights by many minds,*

without truth there could be no justice

*To close the interests of all,*

and without justice no acceptable law.

With prophetic apprehension he foresaw the possibility of a time when 'banded unions' might persecute opinion, making 'single thought a civil crime' and 'individual freedom mute'. He saw clearly that change was a condition of life. As he wrote at about the same time in a famous passage in his 'Morte d'Arthur', the old order, however great the service it has rendered, must continually give place to the new.

*Lest one good custom should corrupt the world.*

He also saw that great and necessary changes could only be brought about peaceably in a community where some 'diffusive thought' could have

*Time and space to work and spread.*

But freedom must not degenerate into licence. 'Tasks of might' must not be delivered to weakness, and freedom must work as an active agent

*Which, Godlike grasps the triple forks,*
*And, Kinglike, wears the crown.*

It must observe certain fixed principles—'The basis of the soul'—and always be conscious of 'The falsehood of extremes'. Both freedom and power must be founded on love, but love also must have its fixed principles and must be a

*True love turned round on fixed poles*

and no less conscious of the lessons of the past than of the conditions of the present and needs of the future.

In the third of these poems he spoke of the tremendous changes which he felt were threatening the stability and security of Western civilization and of the spirit in which a statesman should strive to meet them:

*E'en now we hear with inward strife*
*A motion toiling in the gloom—*
*The Spirit of the years to come*
*Yearning to mix himself with Life.*

*A slow-develop'd strength awaits*
*Completion in a painful school;*
*Phantoms of other forms of rule,*
*New Majesties of mighty States—*

*The warders of the growing hour,*
*But vague in vapour, hard to mark;*
*And round them sea and air are dark*
*With great contrivances of Power.*

*Oh yet, if Nature's evil star*
*Drive men in manhood, as in youth,*
*To follow flying steps of Truth*
*Across the brazen bridge of war—*

*If New and Old, disastrous feud,*
*Must ever shock, like armed foes,*
*And this be true, till Time shall close,*
*That Principles are rain'd in blood;*

*Not yet the wise of heart would cease*
*To hold his hope thro' shame and guilt,*
*But with his hand against the hilt,*
*Would pace the troubled land, like Peace;*

*Not less, tho' dogs of Faction bay,*
*Would serve his kind in deed and word,*
*Certain, if knowledge bring the sword,*
*That knowledge takes the sword away—*

*Would love the gleam of good that broke*
*From either side, nor veil his eyes:*
*And if some dreadful need should rise*
*Would strike, and firmly, and one stroke:*

This idea of the imminence of world-wide revolutionary change haunted him all his life in different forms and with different degrees of apprehension.

The loss of his friend turned Tennyson's mind to more fundamental questions. For four years he remained in seclusion at Somersby, studying history, natural science, metaphysics and theology and striving to perfect himself in the art of poetry to which he had long determined to devote his life. Then at the end of 1837 the house at Somersby had to be given up, and the family moved to High Beech, near Epping. This change brought Tennyson into close contact with some of his Cambridge friends, and through one of them, Richard Monckton Milnes, with many of the leaders of contemporary thought, particularly Thomas Carlyle. The effect of this was to turn his mind once more to political and social problems. His volumes of 1842 gave little sign of this, for most of the poems which they contained had been written or conceived before the move from Lincolnshire. But there are some remarkable instances of the Poet's political prescience in 'Locksley Hall'. I refer not only to the famous anticipation of aerial commerce and warfare and the establishment of universal peace through

*The Parliament of man, the Federation of the world.*

An even more remarkable anticipation occurred in the lines in which Tennyson expressed his fear of the growth of material knowledge without a proportionate increase in the moral sense, and the danger of the standardization of human personality through an egalitarian policy.

*Knowledge comes and wisdom lingers and I linger on the shore*
*And the individual withers and the world is more and more.*

He had, in fact, already expressed the first idea more obscurely in the introductory lines to 'The Palace of Art,' published in 1832:

*Beauty, Good and Knowledge are three sisters*
*That never can be sundered without tears.*
*And he that shuts out Love in turn shall be*
*Shut out from Love and on her threshold lie*
*Howling in outer darkness.*

and he gave it fuller expression in Section CXIV of *In Memoriam* (written probably during the late 1840s), where he says of Knowledge:

> *What is she, cut from love and faith,*
> *But some wild Pallas from the brain*
>
> *Of Demons? fiery-hot to burst*
> *All barriers in her onward race*
> *For power. Let her know her place;*
> *She is the second, not the first.*

The publication of the two volumes of 1842 was followed by a period of misfortune, ill health and nervous prostration, during which Tennyson wrote little and saw little of his friends. But when, in September 1845, his financial position and nervous health were partly restored by the grant of a small pension from the Civil List, he immediately began writing again, and the first poem he published, 'The Golden Year', showed that he was fully alive to the political importance of the time, and perhaps rather ashamed of himself for having stood aloof from the movement of contemporary thought for so long. The poem was published during the intense controversy which raged about Peel's decision to repeal the Corn Laws, and left no doubt that Tennyson's sympathies were entirely with Peel, for the hero, when bantered by his friends because

> *They said he lived shut up within himself,*
> *A tongue-tied poet in these feverous days.*

breaks out in an enthusiastic song in which he looks forward to the time:

> *When wealth no more shall rest in mounded heaps,*
> *But smit with freer light shall slowly melt*
> *In many streams to fatten lower lands,*
> *And light shall spread, and man be liker man*
> *Thro' all the season of the golden year.*

when universal peace shall

> *Lie like a shaft of light across the land*

and the new commerce shall

> *Knit land to land, and blowing havenward*
> *With silks, and fruits, and spices, clear of toll,*
> *Enrich the markets of the golden year.*

But much the most important work undertaken by Tennyson at this time was *The Princess*, a long poem in blank verse, dealing with the education and social status of women. In 1846 the provision for the higher education of women was negligible. The possibility of giving them the Parliamentary franchise had scarcely even been considered, and practically all professions were closed to them. Tennyson had long been keenly interested in the subject, considering that the higher education of women was one of the most important questions confronting the time, and his interest had no doubt been stimulated by his friendship with F. D. Maurice, who was to found Queen's College for Girls in 1848. The way in which he handled the subject was highly characteristic and was, in fact, the only way in which he, as a creative artist, could have handled it, although the result has been to cause a good deal of misinterpretation of his own views. He adopted a purely dramatic method, giving no direct expression of his own opinions, but allowing the various points of view to find utterance entirely through the acts and words of the characters in the story. As a result it is impossible to prove definitely that any view expressed in the poem is or is not the Poet's own view, and he has been saddled with some which he would certainly have repudiated. Indeed, I seem to remember one critic identifying his views with those of the 'maiden aunt', whom the poem describes with genial irony as 'crammed with theories out of books' and 'preaching a universal culture for the crowd'. More frequently the poet is credited with the opinions which he puts into the mouth of that tough old Blimp, the Prince's father:

> *Man for the field and woman for the hearth;*
> *Man for the sword and for the needle she:*
> *Man with the head and woman with the heart:*
> *Man to command and woman to obey:*
> *All else confusion.*

One can, however, see clearly enough with which of the characters Tennyson's sympathies lay, and thus infer with reasonable certainty what his own opinions were. First of all one cannot help being impressed by his obvious sympathy with the Princess herself and her chief supporter, Lady Psyche. The following sayings of the Princess clearly come straight from Tennyson's own heart. From Canto II:

*Knowledge is now no more a fountain seal'd:*
*Drink deep until the habits of the slave,*
*The sins of emptiness, gossip and spite*
*And slander, die. Better not be at all*
*Than not be noble.*

From Canto III:

*Howe'er you babble, great deeds cannot die;*
*They with the sun and moon renew their light*
*For ever, blessing those that look on them—*

also the Princess' claim in Canto IV that women should be

*Not vassals to be beat, nor pretty babes*
*To be dandled, no, but living wills, and sphered*
*Whole in ourselves and owed to none.*

It is noticeable also that in the second Canto he puts into the mouth of the Princess one of the finest of his own statements about time and eternity

*For was, and is, and will be, are but is;*
*And all creation is one act at once,*
*The birth of light, etc.*

Very clear too is Tennyson's voice in the lines which he gives to Lady Psyche in Canto II:

*everywhere*
*Two heads in council, two beside the hearth,*
*Two in the tangled business of the world,*
*Two in the liberal offices of life,*
*Two plummets dropt for one to sound the abyss*
*Of science, and the secrets of the mind:*

*Musician, painter, sculptor, critic, more:*
*And everywhere the broad and bounteous Earth*
*Should bear a double growth of those rare souls,*
*Poets, whose thoughts enrich the blood of the world.*

No doubt the Prince's speeches are the most directly expressive of Tennyson's own views, particularly the description of marriage in Canto VII:

*. . . . . . . . either sex alone*
*Is half itself, and in true marriage lies*
*Nor equal, nor unequal: each fulfils*
*Defect in each, and always thought in thought,*
*Purpose in purpose, will in will, they grow,*
*The single pure and perfect animal,*
*The two-celled heart beating, with one full stroke,*
*Life*

and the long speech which precedes it:

*The woman's cause is man's; they rise or sink*
*Together, dwarf'd or godlike, bond or free. . . .*
*We two will serve them both in aiding her—*
*Will clear away the parasitic forms*
*That seem to keep her up but drag her down—*
*Will leave her space to burgeon out of all*
*Within her—let her make herself her own*
*To give or keep, to live and learn and be*
*All that not harms distinctive womanhood.*
*For woman is not undevelopt man,*
*But diverse: could we make her as the man,*
*Sweet love were slain: his dearest bond is this,*
*Not like to like, but like in difference.*
*Yet in the long years liker must they grow:*
*The man be more of woman, she of man;*
*He gain in sweetness and in moral height,*
*Nor lose the wrestling thews that throw the world;*
*She mental breadth, nor fail in childward care,*
*Nor lose the childlike in the larger mind:*
*Till at the last she set herself to man,*
*Like perfect music unto noble words;*

*And so these twain, upon the skirts of Time,*
*Sit side by side, full-summ'd in all their powers,*
*Dispensing harvest, sowing the To-be,*
*Self-reverent each and reverencing each,*
*Distinct in individualities,*
*But like each other ev'n as those who love.*
*Then comes the statelier Eden back to men:*
*Then reign the world's great bridals, chaste and calm:*
*Then springs the crowning race of human-kind.*

It seems clear from these lines that Tennyson believed woman's capacities to be fully equal, though not entirely similar, to man's and that he approved of their being given the fullest development and expression, so long as woman's prime function, as wife, mother and High Priestess of Domestic Culture, is not impaired.

In the light of what I have said above it is rather difficult to see why modern critics find Tennyson's views on this subject so uncongenial. Mr. Eliot, for example, in his essay on *In Memoriam* (*Selected Essays*, p. 328), refers to 'exasperating views on matrimony, celibacy and female education'. Possibly the suggestion that woman should set herself to man

*Like perfect music unto noble words*

is thought to imply some ineradicable inferiority in woman, although the whole tendency of the rest of the passage is to imply a fundamental equality. In my view the simile is only meant to indicate the differing qualities of the male and female mind and not to suggest any superiority in the male. Possibly modern opinion is repelled by the importance impliedly attached to woman's domestic function and by the reference to the chastity and calm of the ideal sexual relation.

These, however, are points on which it seems possible that time will justify the poet's conclusions rather than the views of his critics.

Three years after the publication of *The Princess* came an event which inevitably brought Tennyson into even closer contact with contemporary politics—his appointment as Poet Laureate in the autumn of 1850. He had always been an admirer of the Queen and a firm believer in the Constitutional Monarchy which was to evolve under, and sometimes in spite of, her leadership. The revolutions that had shaken so many thrones in 1848, and our own abortive Chartist movement, had intensified this faith, and his first poem as Laureate—the address 'To the Queen' prefixed to the edition of his poems issued in 1851—made nobly clear the principles upon which his political creed was founded:

> *. . . May you rule us long,*
> *And leave us rulers of your blood*
> *As noble till the latest day!*
> *May children of our children say,*
> *'She wrought her people lasting good;*
>
> *'Her court was pure; her life serene;*
> *God gave her peace; her land reposed;*
> *A thousand claims to reverence closed*
> *In her as Mother, Wife and Queen;*
>
> *'And statesmen at her council met*
> *Who knew the season when to take*
> *Occasion by the hand, and make*
> *The bounds of freedom wider yet*
>
> *'By shaping some august decree,*
> *Which kept her throne unshaken still,*
> *Broad-based upon her people's will,*
> *And compass'd by the inviolate sea.'*

It was not long before the reign of peace, for which the Poet had prayed, seemed to be rudely threatened. In December 1851, Louis Napoleon made his *coup d'état*, revived the French Empire and assumed the title of Emperor. The effect on many people in England was to renew feelings of apprehension and hostility which had slumbered since Waterloo. Tennyson had been alarmed by the 1848 Revolution in Paris and had inserted a cautionary reference to it in the Epilogue to the third edition of *The Princess* (1850). He now began to fear the renewal of the old Napoleonic pattern, the 'tyranny of all' leading backward to 'the tyranny of one' (*Tiresias*), and in order to rouse the country to a sense of its danger and lack of military preparation, published a number of poems in the Press, one ('For the Penny Wise') in *Fraser's Magazine* and three in *The Examiner*, of which his friend, John Forster, was Editor. Of these, 'Britons, Guard Your Own' appeared on January 31, 1852; 'The Third of February', addressed to the House of Lords on their rejection of Lord John Russell's Militia Bill, and 'Hands All Round' on February 7; and some 'Lines Suggested by Reading an Article in a Newspaper' on February 14. All these poems were published under assumed names because Tennyson feared that their appearance over the name of the Laureate might embarrass the Queen in her relations with Napoleon. The first two were signed 'Merlin', and it is evidence of the care Tennyson took to cover his tracks that the third, which professed to be written in admiration of the first two, began:

*How much I love this writer's manly style*

and was printed over the signature 'Taliessin'.[1]

Although these poems have little significance today, they contain some spirited writing and had considerable effect at the time, greatly stimulating the Volunteer movement. Tennyson himself put his whole heart into them, writing 'Hands All Round' with the tears streaming down his face. That poem was indeed much the best of the series, and it deserves to be remembered if only for its last two stanzas in which the Poet prophetically called on the United States of America to stand by Britain if Europe should once again be involved in war.

*Gigantic daughter of the West,*
*We drink to thee across the flood,*
*We know thee most, we love thee best,*
*For art not thou of British blood?*
*Should war's mad blast again be blown,*
*Permit not thou the tyrant powers*
*To fight thy mother here alone,*
*But let thy broadsides roar with ours.*
*Hands all round!*

[1] In my Biography *Alfred Tennyson* I mentioned doubts which have been expressed as to the authorship of this poem. I have since seen the proofs corrected by Tennyson in his own hand.

*God the tyrant's cause confound!*
*To our great kinsmen of the West, my friends:*
*And the great name of England round and round.*

In September the aged Duke of Wellington, who only three months before had been fighting to secure the enactment of the Militia Bill, died, and Tennyson, who all his life had reverenced him as the saviour of Europe from the tyranny of Napoleon, composed the famous memorial Ode, in which he defined, as he had done twenty years before, his conception of the true freedom:

*That sober freedom out of which there springs*
*Our loyal passion for our temperate Kings,*

and once more warned the nation of the dangers of unpreparedness:

*Remember him who led your hosts;*
*He bad you guard the sacred coasts.*
*Your cannons moulder on the seaward wall,*
*His voice is silent in your council hall*
*For ever; and whatever tempests lour*
*For ever silent; even if they broke*
*In thunder silent; yet remember all*
*He spoke among you, and the Man who spoke;*

Within eighteen months Britain had drifted into war—not against the French, but in alliance with France against Russia—and, in spite of his warnings, lamentably unprepared.

A new factor now began to influence Tennyson's thought. The publication of *In Memoriam* had brought him into close relations with Charles Kingsley, then fiercely engaged with F. D. Maurice in the promotion of the Christian Socialist movement. His talks with these two men deeply impressed upon him the appalling conditions forced on the urban populations by the Industrial Revolution, the continuance of these conditions he felt to be due to the commercial spirit of the age and the Liberal doctrine of *laissez-faire*; and the same causes seemed to him responsible for the country's reluctance to face the duty of national defence and for the new spirit of materialism which was beginning to make itself felt:

*Tho' niggard throats of Manchester may bawl*

he had written in his lines on February 3, 1852:

*What England was shall her true sons forget?*
*We are not cotton spinners all,*
*But some love England's honour yet.*

and in the 'Taliessin' verses he had spoken of 'The British goddess, sleek Respectability', to whom:

*a little feeling is a want of tact,*

and of the new type of British youth:

*. . . so clever yet so small,*
*Thin dilettanti deep in Nature's plan,*
*Who make the emphatic One, by whom is all,*
*An essence less concentred than a man.*

In the summer of 1855, when the unfortunate Crimean War was in full swing, he staggered the literary and political world by the publication of *Maud*, in which he challenged the Liberals with a savage attack on the commercial system and with what appeared to be a eulogy of war. *Maud* is the tragedy of a morbid boy whose father has committed suicide after having been ruined by the fraud of a wealthy neighbour. He lives on in the old family home brooding on his own misery and his father's wrongs, with which the social iniquities of contemporary Britain become linked in his mind. His father's betrayer comes back to live in the neighbourhood with his daughter, Maud. He falls in love with her; the brother opposes the match; a duel results in which the brother is killed. Maud's lover flies the country; she dies and he loses his reason, and when at last he emerges from madness finds reintegration of spirit by volunteering for the war.

In *Maud*, even more than in *The Princess*, one has to remember that the treatment is dramatic, and all the opinions expressed must not be assumed to represent the Poet's own views. The hero is a hypersensitive youth living in morbid solitude. When he speaks of the Peace of the 1850s as being viler than any war,

*Peace sitting under her olive, and slurring the days gone by,*
*When the poor are hovell'd and hustled together, each sex, like swine,*
*When only the ledger lives, and when only not all men lie;*
*Peace in her vineyard—yes!—but a company forges the wine.*

his views—although no doubt they represent Tennyson's sympathies—are not Tennyson's views as he himself would have expressed them in cold blood; nor when the young man says of the Crimean War:

*Let it go or stay, so I wake to the higher aims*
*Of a land that has lost for a little her lust of gold,*
*And love of a peace that was full of wrongs and shames,*
*Horrible, hateful, monstrous, not to be told. . . .*

is Tennyson approving the Crimean War or advocating war as a good thing in itself.[1] His real view about war he expressed clearly again and again, e.g. in the lines from 'Locksley Hall', and those 'To the Queen' (1851) quoted above; the 'Ode for the Opening of the International Exhibition' of 1862; 'Locksley Hall, Sixty Years After' (1886), the Epilogue to 'The Charge of the Heavy Brigade' (1882) and with more subtlety in Section X of *Maud*:

*This huckster put down war! can he tell*
*Whether war be a cause or a consequence?*
*Put down the passions that make earth Hell!*
*Down with ambition, avarice, pride,*
*Jealousy, down! cut off from the mind*
*The bitter springs of anger and fear. . . .*
*For each is at war with mankind.*

In the more extreme parts of the poem he was speaking in character and expressing the malaise of a generation, which those who are old enough will remember to have been curiously renewed in many young men's minds in 1914. No doubt, too, he

[1] Although Tennyson undoubtedly shared the Country's enthusiasm over British feats of arms at Alma, Inkerman and Balaklava, I have found no indication in correspondence or diaries of his views as to the moral justification for the war. In his lines 'To the Rev. F. D. Maurice' he refers to 'the Northern sin which made a selfish war begin.'

hoped by the violence of his statements to shock the reader into a realization of the social horrors of the time.

However, this kind of discrimination was too subtle for the critics of 1855, and *Maud* was received with a chorus of indignation from the Liberal left.

After this there are, for thirty years, very few direct political references in Tennyson's poems. The Crimean War drew from him the poems on the Charges of the Light and Heavy Brigades (the latter not written till many years later and first published in 1882), the Indian Mutiny produced a fiery little poem on Havelock and the famous ballad on 'The Defence of Lucknow'. During the international tension which followed the Austrian attack on Sardinia in 1859, he published in *The Times* (May 7) a poem entitled 'Riflemen Form!' in which he expressed grave doubts as to the sincerity of Napoleon's friendship for Italy ('How can a despot feel with the Free?') and strongly urged support for the volunteer movement (see *Works*, p. 892). He also wrote a rattling war song for the Navy, called 'Jack Tar' (see *Memoir*, p. 366), but did not publish it as it might have seemed like a call to Britain to join in the war. The International Exhibition Ode of 1862 showed that he still had faith in Free Trade as the great missionary of civilization and peace, though this faith was less optimistic than it had been in Peel's time

> *Is the goal so far away?*
> *Far, how far no tongue can say,*
> *Let us dream our dream today.*

But for the most part his energies during these years had a religious and ethical bias. One reason for this was his increasing alarm at the growth of agnosticism and atheism, and what he considered to be the gradual weakening of moral standards. In Section CXXVII of *In Memoriam* he had been able to face with optimism the tendency towards political and social revolution.

> *And all is well, tho' faith and form*
> *Be sunder'd in the night of fear;*
> *Well roars the storm to those that hear*
> *A deeper voice across the storm,*

*Proclaiming social truth shall spread,*
*And justice, ev'n tho' thrice again*
*The red fool-fury of the Seine*
*Should pile her barricades with dead.*

*But ill for him that wears a crown,*
*And him, the lazar, in his rags:*
*They tremble, the sustaining crags;*
*The spires of ice are toppled down,*

*And molten up, and roar in flood;*[1]
*The fortress crashes from on high,*
*The brute earth lightens to the sky,*
*And the great Aeon sinks in blood,*

*And compass'd by the fires of Hell;*
*While thou, dear spirit, happy star,*
*O'erlookst the tumult from afar,*
*And smilest, knowing all is well.*

During the next forty years his confidence, though never entirely destroyed, was often severely shaken by what he judged to be a general spiritual degeneration.

The period between 1855 and 1872 was chiefly occupied with the completion of the *Idylls of the King*, a highly symbolical work in which he expressed his most mature thought on human life and ethics. The symbolism of the *Idylls* is too elaborate for discussion in an essay on Tennyson's politics. It will be enough to say that the Poet's main object was to emphasize the vital importance for men and nations of maintaining a spiritual ideal, and the danger of this succumbing to the combined forces of sensuality and materialism, as Arthur's ideal polity did, in the 'last weird battle of the West'. Yet the poem ends on a note of hope, for Sir Bedivere, watching from the top of the crag the barge which carries the wounded king away to the island of Avilion, hears:

[1] In Canto IV of *The Princess*, no doubt written shortly before this passage, he had described, with similar acceptance, 'Thrones of human Empire' passing like icebergs down the stream of Time and melting into clouds on the horizon—'For all things serve their time'.

*As from beyond the limits of the world,*
*Like the last echo born of a great cry,*
*Sounds, as if some fair city were one voice*
*About a king returning from his wars.*

and while he strains his eyes to watch the barge pass on:

*From less to less and vanish into light*

he sees:

*The new sun rise bringing the new year.*

Early in 1872 Tennyson added, in Strahan's 'Library' Edition of his works, an Epilogue to the Queen, in which he made clear the application of his Arthurian allegory to the problems of the time, which, he says, seemed to many seriously menaced by

*. . . . fierce or careless looseners of the faith,*
*And Softness breeding scorn of simple life,*
*Or Cowardice, the child of lust for gold,*
*Or Labour, with a groan and not a voice,*
*Or Art with poisonous honey stol'n from France,*
*And that which knows, but careful for itself,*
*And that which knows not, ruling that which knows*
*To its own harm: the goal of this great world*
*Lies beyond sight: yet—if our slowly-grown*
*And crown'd Republic's crowning common-sense,*
*That saved her many times, not fail—their fears*
*Are morning shadows huger than the shapes*
*That cast them, not those gloomier which forego*
*The darkness of that battle in the West,*
*Where all of high and holy dies away.*

With the *Idylls* completed, Tennyson turned his attention to the stage and devoted the next ten years to an attempt to establish himself as a poetic dramatist.

Of the seven plays which he completed during these years the historical dramas, *Queen Mary*, *Harold* and *Becket*, had some contemporary relevance, for they dealt with the age-long controversy between England and the Roman Church, which had been passing through a new phase since the emancipation of the Catholics in 1829. During the succeeding fifty years the number of

Catholic priests and chapels in Britain had, to the alarm of the Protestant sects, increased fourfold. In 1850, Cardinal Archbishop Wiseman created a violent uproar by a statement which was thought (absurdly enough) to claim civil jurisdiction for the Catholic See of Westminster. A ridiculous Bill which was passed by Parliament making liable to a fine of £100 anyone who used the offending titles, showed the length to which Protestant panic could go. In 1864, the Pope by an Encyclical specifically condemned every claim to put the civil authority on a level with the ecclesiastical, and anathematized the doctrine that 'the Roman Pontiff should or ought to reconcile or come to terms with progress, liberalism or modern civilization'. Six years later an Oecumenical Council confirmed by solemn decree the dogma of Papal infallibility.

In 1874, when Tennyson began *Queen Mary*, the excitement created by these events was still seething. Although he had at least two intimate friends among the Catholics, Aubrey de Vere and W. G. Ward, whose devotion to their faith he sincerely respected, there can be no doubt that his own sympathy in these controversies was with the Protestants. But his treatment showed a true historical perspective, giving the greater share of his sympathy to Becket in his struggle against the secular encroachment of Henry, and recognizing, in a telling speech given to Lord William Howard in *Queen Mary*, IV, 3, the responsibility attaching to the Protestant prosecution of Catholics:

*Have I not heard them mock the blessed Host*
*In songs so lewd, the beast might roar his claim*
*To being in God's image, more than they?*
*Have I not seen the gamekeeper, the groom,*
*Gardener, and huntsman, in the parson's place,*
*The parson from his own spire swung out dead,*
*And Ignorance crying in the streets, and all men*
*Regarding her? I say they have drawn the fire*
*On their own heads: yet, Paget, I do hold*
*The Catholic, if he have the greater right,*
*Hath been the crueller.*

On the whole these three plays can hardly be said to have had any direct bearing on the controversy of the 1870s. It was rather that this controversy aroused Tennyson's interest in the historical struggle and its dramatic possibilities.

Indeed, he was too little sectarian in his views and too conscious of the inevitable effects of:

> *. . . action and reaction,*
> *The miserable see-saw of our child-world.*

to treat the subject in any but a detached spirit; and towards the end of *Queen Mary* (v, 4), in a startling little vignette he sets the great religious conflict, so savage and of such overwhelming significance to the participants, in a new perspective. Two Protestants are talking in the street outside the Palace where the Queen lies dying. They curse the cruelties of the party of which she has been the leader—'There should be something fierier than fire to yield them their deserts,' says one of the watchers. Suddenly out of the darkness comes a third voice:

THIRD: Deserts . . . whose deserts? Yours? You have a gold ring on your finger, and soft raiment about your body; and is not the woman up yonder sleeping, after all she has done, in peace and quietness, on a soft bed, in a closed room with light, fire, physic, tendance, and I have seen the true men of Christ lying famine-dead by scores, and under no ceiling but the cloud that wept on them, not for them.

FIRST: Friend, tho' so late, it is not safe to preach.
You had best go home. What are you?

THIRD: What am I? One who cries continually with sweat and tears to the Lord God that it would please Him out of His infinite love to break down all kingship and queenship, all priesthood and prelacy, to cancel and abolish all bonds of human allegiance, all the magistracy, all the nobles, and all the wealthy; and to send us again, according to His promise, the one King, the Christ, and all things in common, as in the day of the first church, when Christ Jesus was King.

FIRST: If ever I heard a madman—let's away!
Why, you long-winded—Sir, you go beyond me.
I pride myself on being moderate.
Good night! Go home. Besides, you curse so loud,
The watch will hear you. Get you home at once.

The last and least successful of his plays, 'The Promise of May', completed in 1882, was undoubtedly in large measure designed as an attack on the new spirit of materialism, the growth of which during the 1870s and 1880s filled Tennyson with increasing alarm, and on the new revolutionary creeds of Communism, Nihilism and Anarchism, which were beginning to force themselves on public attention—'Utopian idiocies' which, in the curiously prophetic words of one of the characters in the play:

> *Strangle each other, die, and make the soil*
> *For Caesars, Cromwells, and Napoleons*
> *To root their power in.*

The speaker is the villain of the piece; but I think in this case he was expressing Tennyson's own opinions.

The play, when presented on the stage, aroused the bitter antagonism of the left-wing Radicals, and lacking the artistic merit that might have saved it from failure, had to be withdrawn after a short run.

During these closing years of his life Tennyson found himself, politically, in an extremely uneasy position. He had for many years had a great admiration and affection for Gladstone, who had been Arthur Hallam's closest friend at Eton and Peel's protégé, and whose policy on religious questions and on the protection of small nations he cordially approved. The two men had often been together in London in the 1860s when Gladstone was Chancellor of the Exchequer under Palmerston, and I have found no evidence that Tennyson's confidence was shaken by Gladstone's first Premiership (1868-74), although this saw the initiation of his Irish policy in the Bills to deal with the Land question, to disestablish the Irish Church and to found a Catholic University. When Gladstone dissolved Parliament early in 1874 Tennyson wrote him a sympathetic letter (*Memoir*, p. 548) which, while admitting differences of opinion, commended the great work which he had done and said that, even if he now rested, his name would 'be read in one of the fairest pages of English history'. Disraeli, who succeeded Gladstone in 1874, Tennyson neither liked nor trusted, though in principle he approved his Imperial policy, feeling that a strong and united British Empire, based on Britain's Constitutional Monarchy, was the surest safeguard against a world-wide materialist revolution.

In his Epilogue 'To the Queen' (1872) he had violently attacked an article in a leading London paper suggesting that the connexion with Canada should be severed because of the expense to which it exposed the Mother Country. When in 1882 he re-wrote his poem 'Hands All Round' (first published in 1852), to be sung throughout the Empire on the Queen's birthday, he pleaded strongly for the solidarity of British territories all over the world under the leadership of the Mother Country:

*Pray God our greatness may not fail*
*Thro' craven fears of being great.*

He struck the same note in his lines for the 'Opening of the Indian and Colonial Exhibition' in 1886. As early as 1881 he was in correspondence with the Australian Prime Minister, advocating the Federation of the Australian States, and he often spoke of the need for some kind of Federal Parliament for the Empire. But although he feared and detested Russia, he strongly disapproved of Disraeli's Near Eastern policy, which put Britain in the ignominious position of supporting the Turks against the Christians in the Balkan peninsula, and, after talks with John Bright and Gladstone, he contributed to the *Nineteenth Century* of May 1877 a stirring sonnet in support of the revolutionary Montenegrins.

But Gladstone's administration of 1880–85 was to arouse his violent antagonism.

In 1877 Lord Beaconsfield had annexed the Boer State of the Transvaal in order to save the Dutch from being overwhelmed by their Zulu neighbours. By 1880 all danger from the Zulus was at an end and the Boers rebelled against Britain, finally inflicting a disgraceful defeat on the British forces at Majuba. Gladstone at first refused to treat with the rebels, but afterwards came to the conclusion that they were a small nation whose struggle for emancipation was entitled to respect, and that to continue hostilities against them might bring the Cape Dutch to their assistance. He therefore recognized their independence under very vague terms of suzerainty. I have not found any evidence of Tennyson's reaction to these events, but it is not likely to have been favourable. Nor was Gladstone's Far Eastern policy more likely to appeal to his strong Imperialism. While there seemed a possibility of war between England and Russia arising out of the Russo-Turkish War of 1877-78, the Tsar had sent a mission to Cabul to enlist the support of the Amir of Afghanistan against Britain. Lord Lytton, Viceroy of India, a protégé of Lord Beaconsfield and a strong Imperialist, to whom Tennyson had a few months before dedicated his drama *Harold*, declared war on the Amir, and after some exciting months Lord Roberts brought this to a completely successful close by his victory at Kandahar. Lord Lytton would have liked to annex a large part of Afghanistan, for the defence of India from the North, but Gladstone, who had, meanwhile, come into power, recalled both him and the British Expeditionary Force, installing the late Amir's nephew as ruler. Here again there is no evidence of Tennyson's reactions. It is however certain that Gladstone's Irish policy soon began to cause him serious uneasiness. When, in the spring of 1881, his friend, the Duke of Argyll, resigned from the Government as a protest against what he considered the unsound economics of Gladstone's Irish Land Bill, Tennyson addressed to him some rather enigmatic lines, which might be interpreted as approving the Duke's independence of spirit without endorsing the reason for which he had acted:

*O Patriot Statesman, be thou wise to know*
*The limits of resistance, and the bounds*
*Determining concession; still be bold*
*Not only to slight praise but suffer scorn;*
*And be thy heart a fortress to maintain*
*The day against the moment, and the year*
*Against the day: thy voice, a music heard*
*Thro' all the yells and counter-yells of feud*
*And faction, and thy will, a power to make*
*This ever-changing world of circumstance,*
*In changing, chime with never-changing Law.*

Probably these lines were deliberately ambiguous, as Tennyson felt it inconsistent with his position, as the Laureate of a Constitutional Monarch, to engage in party politics.

In May of the next year, the murder in Dublin of Lord Frederick Cavendish and Mr. Burke seemed to confirm the worst fears of those who opposed Gladstone's policy, and although he had the courage immediately to introduce a stringent Crimes Bill to enable the Government to deal more effectively with such outrages, the good effect of this was, to some extent, offset by the release of Parnell and his colleagues from Kilmainham Gaol.

Still, the Crimes Bill was a sign of grace and the Prime Minister's friends were further reassured by the strong line which he took with regard to Arabi's rebellion in Egypt. The construction of the Suez Canal by the French engineer de Lesseps in 1869-70 had vitally changed the conditions of Eastern trade and introduced new political considerations of the first importance. In 1875 Disraeli had bought approximately a half share in the Canal Company, and ever since then Britain and France had exercised a kind of unauthorized dominion over Egypt. In 1879 the Khedive was compelled to put the whole financial control of his country in the hands of a British Minister and a French Minister nominated by their respective Governments. This dual control aroused great discontent among the Egyptian officials and ministers, and in 1882 Arabi Pasha raised the cry of 'Egypt for the Egyptians!', executed a *coup d'état* and seized the person of the Khedive. The French refused to take any action and Gladstone hesitated until, in June 1882, a riot broke out in Alexandria, which resulted in the massacre of a considerable number of Europeans. Gladstone now acted promptly and with decisive effect. Admiral Seymour bombarded and occupied Alexandria, and Sir Garnet Wolseley completely defeated Arabi at Tel-el-Kebir in September 1882.

In all this, no doubt Gladstone had the warm approval of Tennyson, who celebrated Wolseley's victory with an enthusiastic reference in the Prologue to 'The Charge of the Heavy Brigade'.

Relations between the two men were sufficiently good in 1883 for Tennyson to accept an invitation to join Gladstone and his family in a yachting cruise, in the *Pembroke Castle*, round the North Coast of Scotland to Denmark. At Kirkwall they both received the freedom of the City, and at Copenhagen entertained the King and Queen of Denmark, the Tsar and Tsarina, and the King and Queen of Greece on board the ship. On the way home across the North Sea, Gladstone—probably acting on a suggestion from Queen Victoria—offered Tennyson a peerage, which, after much hesitation, he accepted, partly out of courtesy to the Queen and partly because he did not feel that he would be justified in refusing the offer, for himself and his descendants, of a seat in what he considered the finest legislative assembly in the world. He took his seat on the cross-benches to show that he owed allegiance to neither party, and in December, as though to make public profession of the principles on which he intended to act, published in *Macmillan's Magazine* a poem, entitled 'Freedom', in which, while declaring his devotion to the

> *Golden dream*
> *Of knowledge fusing class with class,*
> *Of civic hate no more to be,*
> *Of love to leaven all the mass,*
> *Till every soul be free,*

he strongly deprecated any precipitate action which might

> *. . . mar*
> *By changes all too fierce and fast*
> *This order of her human star,*
> *This heritage of the past*

concluding with two stanzas against demagogues:

> *Men loud against all forms of power—*
> *Unfurnished brows, tempestuous tongues—*
> *Expecting all things in an hour*
> *Brass mouths and iron lungs.*

The closing lines may perhaps have been aimed at the Irish agitators, for I do not think these years were remarkable for mass oratory in England. In fact, the last stanza had been written in reference to the Reform troubles about fifty years before, though never published, and it may be that the poet's pleasure in being able to make use of it at last rather blinded him to its comparative irrelevance.

Although Tennyson, when he accepted the peerage, had intended to keep altogether clear of party controversy, he very soon found himself drawn into it by his friendship with Gladstone. In February 1884, Gladstone introduced a Franchise Bill which aimed at increasing the Electorate from three to five million by a considerable enfranchisement of the agricultural voter, and, during the progress of the Bill through the Commons, pledged himself—if it became law—to bring in a redistribution Bill before Parliament was dissolved. When the Bill came before the Lords, the Opposition introduced an amendment which would have had the effect of suspending the Bill until the scheme of Redistribution was introduced. Gladstone called on Tennyson to vote against this amendment. Tennyson was by no means enthusiastic about wide extensions of the franchise for a nation which had only enjoyed a national scheme of primary education for thirteen years, and had as yet no national secondary education; but he realized that as both parties had taken part in franchise extension (the Conservatives by Disraeli's Reform Act of 1866), it would be dangerous to block the passage of Gladstone's Bill. At the same time, he felt strongly the justice of the claim that so large and fundamental a change should be accompanied by a redistribution, which would settle on equitable terms the rival claims of town and country voters, Northern and Southern Ireland, and so on. He therefore replied to Gladstone that, though he could not vote with him he would not vote against him, but promised that if the Government pledged themselves not to pass the Franchise Bill until the terms of the Redistribution had been satisfactorily settled, he would support them.

The Opposition amendment was carried, and, as subsequent negotiations between the parties failed, the prorogation of Parliament at the end of the month killed the Bill.

As soon as Parliament reassembled in the autumn a second Bill was introduced. This came before the Lords on Nov. 13, and Tennyson, who was still determined that Extension and Redistribution should, so far as possible, go forward together, sent the Prime Minister the following lines[1]:

[1] At about this time—probably rather later—Tennyson addressed to Gladstone the lines published under the title 'Politics' in his *Demeter* volume of 1889, and ending with the quatrain:

*For some say 'Quick' and some cry 'Slow',*
*But, while the hills remain,*
*Uphill 'Too slow' will need the whip,*
*Down-hill 'Too quick', the chain.*

*Steersman, be not precipitate in thine act*
*Of steering, for the river here, my friend,*
*Parts in two channels moving to one end—*
*This goes straight forward to the cataract:*
*That streams about the bend.*
*But though the cataract seem the nearer way,*
*Whate'er the crowd on either bank may say,*
*Take thou the bend, 'twill save thee many a day.*

Gladstone demurred at this and on November 16 Tennyson wrote to him again, 'I know nothing of Parliamentary tactics, but I have a strong conviction that the more simple the dealings of men with men and man with man are—the better.' He therefore urged Gladstone to go straight to the House and say, 'When the Lords have passed the second reading of the Franchise Bill, we pledge ourselves to lay on the table our redistribution Bill.' As a result Gladstone made a declaration more or less on these lines, and the Franchise Bill became law before the end of the year.

Reading between the lines of their correspondence on this subject one can, I think, detect a growing uneasiness on Tennyson's part at Gladstone's subtle and circuitous methods of negotiation.

Worse was to come. For some time the Arab tribes in the Egyptian provinces of the Sudan had been in a state of unrest. A fanatic from Dongola, named Mahommed Ahmed, had proclaimed himself the *Mahdi* or Prophet expected by all Mussulmans to appear shortly before the Last Judgment. The tribes rallied round him and drove the Egyptian troops into their fortresses. In October 1883, General Hicks, who had been sent with a hastily improvised force to oppose the rebels, was defeated and his Army cut to pieces. Gladstone, not realizing the fanatical nature of the Mahdi's movement, determined to recognize the tribes as a people not improperly seeking political independence, and sent General Gordon, a popular hero and a friend for whom Tennyson had a profound admiration and affection, to Khartoum to withdraw the Egyptian forces. In February 1884, Gordon was besieged in Khartoum by the insurgents. He had no adequate forces for the defence of the position and sent urgent demands to England for British troops. Gladstone hesitated until the autumn, when he sent Wolseley, the victor of Tel-el-Kebir, to relieve

Khartoum. But it was too late. Wolseley reached Khartoum only to find that the place had fallen and that Gordon, with the whole of his garrison of 11,000 men, had been massacred. The outburst of popular grief at this calamity has hardly ever been paralleled, and the effect on Tennyson's relations with Gladstone could not fail to be severe. When, in April, Britain stood on the brink of war with Russia over Afghanistan, he felt so doubtful of the Government's willingness to defend British interests, that he published in *The Times* of April 22 the savage lines entitled 'The Fleet' (*Works*, p. 577), concluding with the stanza:

> *You, you, that have the ordering of her fleet,*
> *If you should only compass her disgrace,*
> *When all men starve, the wild mob's million feet*
> *Will kick you from your place.*

Five days later Gladstone asked for a credit of £11,000,000, of which 6½ millions were for the Navy, supporting his request with a speech that took the House by storm and swept away all opposition.

On June 12 Gladstone resigned, and it is evidence of Tennyson's strong feeling about the events of the preceding months that he agreed, at the private and personal request of the Queen, to approach him and ask him to carry out his often expressed intention of retiring from politics. If any such approach was made it was unsuccessful, for Gladstone not only stood again but was re-elected with a majority over the Conservatives, but not over them and the Irish together.

Gladstone's introduction of his first Home Rule Bill, in April of the next year (1886), drove Tennyson into open opposition. In spite of his determination not to be drawn into party politics, he sent a message to one of the Liberal opponents of the Bill stigmatizing 'all who tamper with the Union' as 'either madmen or traitors', and urging that a solemn league and covenant should be entered into by members of whatever party, to place country before party and vote against the disruption of the Empire under whatever guise. As late as June 1832, within a few months of his death, he wrote to a correspondent, 'I love Mr. Gladstone, but I hate his Irish policy.'

His feeling against the Prime Minister was now so strong that when he was stopping with Sir James Knowles, in Queen Anne's Gate, and found that Gladstone had been asked to dine, he stoutly refused to meet his old friend and retired to his bedroom, alleging a headache. After dinner, Gladstone insisted on going to see him, in the hope that his headache might be better and he willing to come down. The rest of the party awaited the result with some trepidation; but such was Gladstone's charm and persuasiveness that after a few minutes the two old men were heard shuffling down the stairs together, to spend the rest of the evening comfortably on the sofa, discussing theology and Greek literature.

That summer Gladstone's Government fell. In December, Tennyson, now seventy-seven years old, staggered the English-speaking world with the most surprising poem of his long career, 'Sixty Years After', a sequel to 'Locksley Hall'. In this the hero of the early poem, now an old man of eighty, looks back on the past with all its sorrows and disappointments, the gradual passing of the old social order and the growth of a soulless commercialism. The poem ranges over a wide field involving not only political but also (and mainly) religious and ethical questions, and all these are so closely interlinked that it is practically impossible to disengage them. I have therefore dealt comprehensively with the whole poem in my essay on Tennyson's Religion (see pp. 102-8). Here it will be sufficient to say that 'Sixty Years After' created on the general reader an impression of fierce disillusion—even of a deliberate repudiation of the generally accepted principles of Parliamentary democracy and of all the political and economic progress of the last half century—and caused an even greater stir in the Liberal camp than *Maud* had done thirty years before—so much so indeed that Mr. Gladstone himself took up the challenge with an elaborately deferential article in *The Nineteenth Century* for January 1887. In this he gave an impressive catalogue of the reforms initiated by Parliament since 1842, and expressed the fear that Tennyson's poem might be taken for 'a deliberate authoritative estimate of the time', and this be made an excuse for 'the indulgence of the opposite but often concurring weakness of a carping and also of a morbid temper'. The poem, he maintained, was purely subjective and did not deal with the 'outward' world at all—the poet's imagery being like the perception of colour by the eye, which tells only the individual's personal impression of the thing seen, not of the thing itself.

The old statesman's resentment was most clearly shown in the concluding sentence of his article, in which he referred to the forthcoming celebration of the fiftieth year of Victoria's reign. 'Justice does not require, nay rather she forbids, that the Jubilee of the Queen be marred by tragic notes.'

This was Tennyson's last invasion of the political field. In his 'Ode' for the Queen's Jubilee (1887) he took Gladstone's hint and no tragic note marred his enthusiasm, although he added, with her express approval—possible at her suggestion—the concluding section (XI):

*Are there thunders moaning in the distance . . .*

In the following winter he had a serious illness from which the doctors thought he would not recover. His great strength and vitality pulled him through, but the experience brought the thought of death very near to him and turned his mind to larger issues. With Gladstone out of office the old friendly feelings returned. On Tennyson's recovery from his illness in 1889 and on the publication of *Demeter and Other Poems*, of which he sent Gladstone a copy, affectionate correspondence passed between them. But party politics now began to seem very far away, and the last lines which he wrote on the subject were the following from 'Vastness' (published 1889):

*Raving politics, never at rest—as this poor earth's pale history runs—*
*What is it all but a trouble of ants in the gleam of a million million of suns?*

## III

# *Tennyson's Religion*

TENNYSON GREW to maturity in a period of intense religious ferment, which was destined to continue with varying phases during the whole of his long life. His boyhood and youth saw the development of a strong religious revival which was evangelical in origin but produced, as offshoots or reactions, the Tractarian and Anglo-Catholic movements of the 1830s, and later, under pressure from rationalist attack and scientific discovery, the Broad Church movement.

The Evangelical Revival is said to have reached its peak in 1827, which saw the close of Edward Irving's Hatton Garden Mission and the publication of Keble's famous volume of hymns, *The Christian Year*. It was also the year in which Tennyson went up to Cambridge, after a childhood and adolescence of intense and uneasy religious experience.

His capacity for this was extremely precocious and it seems that he had, while still a boy, attained some of the convictions that were to provide the basis of his religious thought to the end of his life. For example, at the very opening of *The Devil and the Lady*, his early play (written at fourteen), there stands an invocation to Love as the guiding principle of the universe:

> *O thou omnipotent Love, whose boundless sway*
> *And uncontroll'd dominion boweth down*
> *The Spirits of the Mighty, thou great Despot,*
> *Who bindest in thy golden chains the strong*
> *And the imbecile, thou immortal Pan-Arch*
> *Tyrant o' th' earth and sea whose sunless depth*
> *And desolate Abyss is vivified*
> *And quicken'd at thy bidding—thou vast link*
> *Of the Creation—thou deep sentiment!*
> *Thou only to be understood by those*
> *Who feel thee and aid thy purpose. . . .*

This idea is repeated in the early poem 'Love and Death' (first published in 1880), and in the two early Sonnets quoted in Hallam Tennyson's notes (*Works*, pp. 900–1). It recurs throughout Tennyson's work and finds a place in his posthumous volume of 1892, e.g. 'Doubt and Prayer', and 'The Death of the Duke of Clarence and Avondale'. His boyish poems also make it clear that already, before reaching the years of adolescence, he possessed in some degree the power mystics have claimed through the centuries, to establish immediate communication (the description is that of Evelyn Underhill) between the spirit of man, entangled among material things, and that only reality, 'that immaterial and final being which some philosophers call the Absolute and most theologians call God'.

In his early poem 'Armageddon', written at about the same time as *The Devil and the Lady*, he describes, with all the conviction of personal experience, one such moment of direct communication. I quote at length to show the state of spiritual exaltation which accompanied the experience and to make it clear that this was spontaneous and genuine and not in any way derived from literary suggestions. The boy conceives himself as watching, from a height above the Valley of Megiddo, the preparations for the last great battle between the forces of Righteousness and the forces of Evil.

*Eve came down*
*Upon the valleys and the sun was setting;*
*Never set sun with such portentous glare*
*Since he arose on that gay morn, when Earth*
*First drunk the light of his prolific ray.*
*Strange figures thickly thronged his burning orb,*
*Spirits of discord seem'd to weave across*
*His fiery disk a web of bloody haze,*
*Thro' whose reticulations struggled forth*
*His ineffectual, intercepted beams,*
*Curtaining in one dark terrific pall*
*Of dun-red light heaven's azure and earth's green.*

*The beasts fled to their dens; the little birds*
*All wing'd their way home shrieking: fitful gusts*
*Of violent tempest shook the scanty palm*

F

*That cloth'd the mountain ridge whereon I stood;*
*And in the red and murky Even light,*
*Black, formless, unclean things came flitting by;*
*Some seemed of bestial similitude*
*And some half human, yet so horrible,*
*So shadowy, indistinct and undefin'd,*
*It were a mockery to call them ought*
*Save unrealities, which took the form*
*And fashioning of such ill-omened things*
*That it were sin almost to look on them.*

*There was a mingling too of such strange sounds*
*(Which came at times upon my startled hearing)*
*Half wailing and half laughter; such a dissonance*
*Of jarring confus'd voices, part of which*
*Seem'd hellish and part heavenly, whisperings,*
*Low chauntings, strangled screams, and other notes*
*Which I may liken unto nothing which*
*I ever heard on Earth, but seem'd most like*
*A mixture of the voice of man and beast;*
*And then again throughout the lurid waste*
*Of air, a breathless stillness reigned, so deep,*
*So deathlike, so appalling, that I shrunk*
*Into myself again, and almost wish'd*
*For the recurrence of those deadly sounds,*
*Which fixed my senses into stone, and drove*
*The buoyant life-drops back into my heart.*

In the East he sees the encampment of the forces of God:

*Ranges of silver tents beside the moon*

and

*Full opposite within the lurid West,*
*In clear relief against the long rich vein*
*Of melancholy red that fring'd the sky,*
*A suite of dark pavilions*

where lurk the forces of evil.

Suddenly a seraph stands beside him and bids him open his eyes and see. The effect upon the boy is strange.

*I look'd, but not*
*Upon his face, for it was wonderful*
*With its exceeding brightness, and the light*
*Of the great Angel Mind that look'd from out*
*The starry glowing of his restless eyes.*
*I felt my soul grow godlike, and my spirit*
*With supernatural excitation bound*
*Within me, and my mental eye grew large*
*With such a vast circumference of thought,*
*That, in my vanity, I seem'd to stand*
*Upon the outward verge and bound alone*
*Of God's omniscience. Each failing sense,*
*As with a momentary flash of light*
*Grew thrillingly distinct and keen.*[1] *I saw*
*The smallest grain that dappled the dark Earth,*
*The indistinctest atom in deep air,*
*The Moon's white cities, and the opal width*
*Of her small, glowing lakes, her silver heights*
*Unvisited with dew of vagrant cloud,*
*And the unsounded, undescended depth*
*Of her black hollows. Nay—the hum of men*
*Or other things talking in unknown tongues,*
*And notes of busy Life in distant worlds,*
*Beat, like a far wave, on my anxious ear.*

*I wondered with deep wonder at myself;*
*My mind seem'd wing'd with knowledge and the strength*
*Of holy musings and immense Ideas,*
*Even to Infinitude. All sense of Time*
*And Being and Place was swallowed up and lost*
*Within a victory of boundless thought.*
*I was a part of the Unchangeable,*
*A scintillation of Eternal Mind,*
*Remix'd and burning with its parent fire.*

[1] *Cf.* the description of Arthur's clairvoyance in 'The Coming of Arthur', (*Works*, p. 310).

There are several references to this experience in Tennyson's later poems, e.g. 'The Mystic', an early poem not published during the poet's lifetime (see *Works*, p. 991); the closing lines of 'The Holy Grail'; and 'Far-Far-Away' (1889). The most interesting, because the most detailed and analytical, description occurs in 'The Ancient Sage' (1889), which I shall quote later.

Another idea which strongly influenced Tennyson all through his life is expressed by the Devil at the beginning of Act II of *The Devil and the Lady*—the reality of the spiritual and the unreality of the material world.

*O suns and spheres and stars and belts and systems,*
*Are ye or are ye not?*
*Are ye realities or semblances*
*Of that which men call real?*
*Are ye true substance? are ye anything*
*Except delusive shows and physical points*
*Endow'd with some repulsive potency?*
*Could the Omnipotent fill all space, if ye*
*Or the least atom in ye or the least*
*Division of that atom (if least can dwell*
*In infinite divisibility) should be impenetrable?*
*I have some doubts if ye exist when none*
*Are by to view ye; if your Being alone*
*Be in the mind and the intelligence*
*Of the created? should some great decree*
*Annihilate the sentient principle*
*Would ye or would ye not be non-existent?*
*'Tis a shrewd doubt—*

In these lines Tennyson seems to be following the principles of Bishop Berkeley. In his later poems, e.g. 'The Higher Pantheism', he pushed his theory further, coming to regard matter as 'merely the shadow of something greater than itself which we poor short-sighted creatures cannot see'. (See p. 109 and Hallam Tennyson's note in first column of *Works*, p. 977,) The supposed infinite divisibility of the atom often exercised his mind. Sixty years later he wrote in 'The Ancient Sage':

*For Knowledge is the swallow on the lake*
*That sees and stirs the surface-shadow there*
*But never yet hath dipt into the abysm,*
*The Abysm of all Abysms, beneath, within*
*The blue of sky and sea, the green of earth,*
*And in the million-millionth of a grain*
*Which cleft and cleft again for evermore,*
*And ever vanishing, never vanisheth,*
*To me, my son, more mystic than myself*
*Or even than the Nameless is to me . . .*

Unfortunately, with the years of adolescence came influences which cruelly disturbed the certainty of the boy's early intuitions. These sprang from the clash between the personalities and beliefs of his parents and the gradually increasing miseries of home life in the Rectory at Somersby. His father, Dr. George Clayton Tennyson, was a parson of the Hanoverian type, distrustful of enthusiasm in all forms and a strong upholder of the political and social pretensions of the Church of England—essentially a scholar and a gentleman, only secondarily a priest. Very different was Alfred's mother, a simple, devout and enthusiastic Evangelical of the pietistic Revival, much nearer to the doctrines of Wesley than to those of Laud. The gradual breakdown of Dr. Tennyson's mental health, which in the end made him a helpless victim of the drink habit, accentuated the differences between him and his wife, and drove Alfred during his boyhood more and more within the scope of her earnest pietism. At first this may have been a source of strength and comfort to him, but before long he felt himself torn not only by a divided loyalty to his parents, to both of whom he was deeply attached, but also by intellectual doubts which grievously shook the foundations of his boyish faith, burdening him with a guilt complex which the circumstances of home life made it difficult for him to shake off. This tendency was, no doubt, increased by his aunt Mary Bourne, the Calvinistic wife of the Squire of Dalby, five miles off on the Wolds. Some of her sayings Tennyson used to repeat with grim amusement in after years. She would weep with emotion at the infinite goodness of God. 'Has He not', she would exclaim, 'damned most of my friends? But *me*, *me* He has picked out for eternal salvation, *me* who am no better than my neighbours!' It seems that she included Alfred among the goats. 'Alfred, Alfred,' she said to him one day, 'when I look at you I think of the words of Holy Scripture, "Depart from me, ye cursed, into everlasting fire".' At the time, however, the influence of Aunt Bourne—whom he described as one of the most wayward and at times violent of human beings—must have been very distressing, helping to produce moods of despair, such as that described in the sonnet in *Early Unpublished Poems* (1931), addressed to some friend or relative who cannot now be identified:

*Sonnet*

*When the rank heat of evil's tropic day*
*Made floating cloud of flowing joy, and cleft*
*My shores of life (their freshness steamed away,*
*Nothing but salt and bitter crystals left),*
*When in my lonely walks I seemed to be*
*An image of the cursed figtree, set*
*In the brown glens of this Mount Olivet,*
*Thy looks, thy words, were sun and rain to me.*
*When all sin-sickened, loathing my disgrace,*
*Far on within the temple of the mind*
*I seemed to hear God speaking audibly,*
*'Let us go hence'—sometimes a little space,*
*Out of the sphere of God, I dared to find*
*A shadow and a resting place in thee.*

Further evidence of his inner conflict is to be found in several of the fragments in the *Early Unpublished Poems* (e.g. 'Memory'; 'Perdidi Diem'), in 'Remorse' (*Poems by Two Brothers*), and more clearly still in the 'Supposed Confessions', which he published in his volume of 1830. The fact that Tennyson made this poem public shows that, after two years at Cambridge and the experience of Arthur Hallam's strengthening friendship, he felt able to view it objectively; but one cannot read it without being convinced that it records emotions which he had actually experienced and which had made a deep and agonizing impression on him. Over it there seems to brood the shadow of the three main principles of the

Evangelical creed—the conviction of original sin, inherited from the fall of Adam, and the consequent doom of mankind to eternal punishment from which salvation is promised to the elect through the atoning death of Christ.

> *Oh God, my God, have mercy now.*
> *I faint, I fall. Men say that thou*
> *Didst die for me, for such as* me,
> *Patient of ill, and death, and scorn,*
> *And that my sin was as a thorn*
> *Among the thorns that girt thy brow*
> *Wounding thy soul. . . .*

But the Poet finds it hard to believe in the efficacy of this promise. He confesses that in his 'extremest misery of ignorance' he longs for some miraculous sign to strengthen his faith. Once he rejoiced in the conviction that man is endowed with free will and with the privilege to doubt and to endeavour to resolve his doubts by free and courageous enquiry. Now he fears that if once he gives way to doubt he will lose the simple faith which he had learned at his mother's knee and which had been his chief refuge from the trials and agonies of his tortured adolescence.

Tennyson's introduction to the stimulating company of 'The Apostles' and his friendship with Arthur Hallam enabled him to shake off this mood. The Apostles had been founded by F. D. Maurice, who had been brought up in a Unitarian household and was destined to become a leader of the Broad Church party, and John Sterling, then a Benthamite with extremely latitudinarian views on religion. Moreover, the Society was, through Connop Thirlwall and Julius Hare, who were resident Fellows of Trinity College, brought into touch with the new school of biblical criticism that had arisen in Germany and was destined to bring about an entirely new conception of the inspiration and infallibility of the Scriptures, up to that time generally regarded as unassailable.

It is clear, however, that Tennyson's liberation was not achieved without a struggle. Hallam himself felt the same difficulties, though his more genial and optimistic nature enabled him to conquer them more easily. See e.g. *In Memoriam*, XCVI:

*He fought his doubts and gathered strength,*
*He would not make his judgment blind,*
*He faced the spectres of the mind*
*And laid them: thus he came at length*
*To find a stronger faith his own;*

Indeed, he went so far as to attempt in his essay 'Theodicaea Novissima', to prove that the eternal punishment of the wicked may not be incompatible with the doctrine of God's sovereign love. This Tennyson's sensitive and highly imaginative temperament was never willing to admit, and before he left Cambridge he had evidently shaken off all traces of the Evangelical tenets of his mother and his Aunt Bourne, no further signs of which appear in the volumes of 1830 and 1832.

Then, in 1833, Arthur Hallam died. Tennyson's immediate reactions to this crushing blow are shown in 'The Two Voices' (with its subsidiary title 'Thoughts of a Suicide'), which he began to write very soon after Hallam's death. In it he touched on some of the ideas which he afterwards elaborated in *In Memoriam*. Its chief interest as an index of Tennyson's religious development is, however, its concentration on the question of personal immortality. There is no longer any hint of the guilt complex which dominated the 'Supposed Confessions', nor is the after life considered as a possible medium of reward or punishment. That phase has passed; but the shock of his loss was so great that for a time Tennyson himself longed for death, and this longing, coupled with his longing for reunion with the spirit of his friend, forced on his mind the mystery of the 'something after death': What are the possibilities of a future life? What can its nature be? And is man justified in seeking refuge in death from the miseries which human life may inflict upon him?

Tennyson began work on *In Memoriam* at about the time he was writing 'The Two Voices', and it represents the progress of his religious thought during the next fifteen or sixteen years. One must not, however, expect from it any logical development of views, or even any closely reasoned statement of beliefs. The various sections of the poem were composed at different times over a long period of years without any idea of welding them into a connected whole. They represent a series of moods, no doubt in a more or less true progression, but some of them mutually contradictory, and the statements of faith or hope which result from these moods are intuitive and emotional, not carefully considered axioms.

The different phases of the poem were, no doubt, strongly influenced by the course of the great theological controversies which continued to rage during the second quarter of the century, and the publication of important scientific discoveries—or alleged discoveries—which seemed to have a bearing on the questions at issue. Early in the 1830s Newman launched the Tractarian movement, which ended in the secession of himself and his friends to Rome in 1844-45. In 1835, Strauss published his famous *Life of Christ*, in which he denied the Redeemer all supernatural attributes, suggesting that the whole Messianic legend had come into being long before the birth of Jesus and had been attached to His personality by subsequent tradition. In 1850, Francis Newman, brother of J. H. Newman, published his *Phases of Faith*, in which he attacked the doctrines of the Trinity, Original Sin, the Atonement and Eternal Punishment, and challenged the historical authority of the Old and New Testaments. Shortly before this, J. S. Mill had brought out his famous *Logic*, in which he restated and elaborated the doctrine of Universal Causation (previously hinted at by other philosophers and clearly stated by Laplace), according to which the condition of the universe at any instant was held to be the consequence of its state at the previous instant, so that if anyone at any instant had a comprehensive knowledge of all the relevant factors, he could foretell the whole of subsequent history. This seemed entirely to exclude the possibility of human free will, human responsibility to the Creator, and any kind of supernatural intervention, whether by miracle, revelation or special providence. In other words, everything was made subject to the rule of Law, with which no external interference was possible.

In the previous year Robert Chambers had published his *Vestiges of the Natural History of Creation*, in which he argued that the formation of the earth as we know it and the development of all the species of living creatures by which it is inhabited have been due to natural physical causes, the higher gradually evolving from the lower, and not to acts of separate creation by a Divine Being. Chambers tried to show 'that the world constituted one vast self-acting machine, by which everything from stellar systems to animalculae was turned out as it was required with universal and undeviating regularity'. He outlined the doctrine of evolution, afterwards elaborated by Darwin, but without having thought of Darwin's principle of Natural Selection.

Chambers's book aroused violent opposition both from the Churches and the more orthodox scientists, but it made an immense impression on thinking people and undoubtedly prepared the way for Darwin's more thorough and scientific work.

Tennyson kept abreast of all these movements and discoveries. He had always a keen appetite for knowledge, and it is clear from *The Devil and the Lady* that even in his boyhood his mind had been familiar with many metaphysical and religious problems. Cambridge and the stimulating company of The Apostles had intensified these interests, and the loss of his friend made stronger than ever his desire for an understanding of the eternal problems relating to the freedom of the human will, the immortality of the human spirit and the object and direction of the universe, the solution of which had been the aim of all the great religious and philosophical systems of the world.

*In Memoriam* shows the course of his speculation on these subjects from the end of 1833 to 1848 or 1849. It is clear that by the time he began work on the poem his mind had moved a considerable distance from the position indicated in the 'Supposed Confessions'. During the years which had passed since the mental struggle depicted in that poem, he had not only become familiar with contemporary scientific and philosophic movements, but had studied the great religions of the world deeply enough to contemplate the composition of an epic poem symbolizing their teachings and implications.

In the 'Supposed Confessions' he had hardly ventured to face 'man's privilege' of doubt. The mere thought of such a responsibility had destroyed all his joy in man's greater privilege of free will, which was so cardinal a point in his creed. In *In Memoriam*, Section XCVI (no doubt written at the end of the 1830s or in the early '40s), he is able to say:

> *There lives more faith in honest doubt,*
> *Believe me, than in half the creeds.*

In the earlier poem the Poet appears profoundly grieved—indeed, almost appalled—at his inability any longer to accept the conventional Christian dogmas. In *In Memoriam*, although two of the most moving sections (XXXI and XXXII)[1] are founded on the raising of Lazarus, there is a marked absence of dogma, and the emphasis seems throughout to be on the humanity of Christ. There is only one passage, outside the Lazarus sections (and possibly the introductory stanzas, see p. 92), in which his divinity seems to be necessarily implied—that is in Section LXXXIV, where Tennyson allows himself to dream of what his life might have been if Arthur had lived. He even imagines that he and Arthur might die together and:

*arrive at last the blessed goal,*
*And He that died in Holy Land*
*Would reach us out the shining hand,*
*And take us as a single soul.*

—a curiously unreal and romantic conception. Elsewhere Tennyson seems to think of Christ as man rather than God. Thus in Section XXXIII (probably written before 1835), when speaking of the importance of doing nothing to disturb a young girl's simple faith, he says:

*Oh sacred be the flesh and blood*
*To which she links a truth divine.*

In XXXVI he writes:

*And so the Word had breath and wrought*
*With human hands the creed of creeds,*

and in the two preceding stanzas of this section he seems to imply that the Gospel story is only symbolic—adapted (perhaps divinely adapted) to convey to limited human understandings a hint of truths which cannot be clearly or fully expressed in human terms. For the personality and reported sayings of Christ he had always a mystical reverence. For example, forty years later when walking on the Down at Farringford with his niece, Agnes Weld, he stopped and, pointing to one of the little wild flowers growing in

[1] It is perhaps significant that these are amongst the earliest sections of the poem—probably composed at the end of 1833.

the short hill turf, said with that simplicity which made his serious utterances so impressive:

'There is not a flower on the Down that owes as much to the sun as I do to Christ.'

But he would not be pinned down to any more dogmatic statement, and he would not go further in describing Christ's Godhead than to agree that He might be in some sort—perhaps not exclusively—an incarnation of the Divine. In the middle 1870s he horrified John Bright by saying that he 'thought the Turkish religion a very good one', and in the remarkable vision, which he inserted, rather incongruously, in 'Sea Dreams' (published in 1864, see *Works*, p. 159), he showed clearly that he regarded the great historic creeds as having purely relative validity and as doomed to vanish and be superseded by others in accordance with the inexorable but wholesome law of spiritual evolution, which may in the end sweep away the basic dogma of the Christian religion itself, for the mystical wave, which in the dream drives across the world, battering down the cliff-like line of

*Huge cathedral fronts of every age*

ends by threatening with destruction the Virgin Mother and her Babe, who stand far up on one of those dark minster fronts:

*Both high among the stars and crowned with stars.*

Judging from the scanty references in *In Memoriam*, one may perhaps infer that by the middle 1830s he had already reached a similar position.[1]

It is not surprising, therefore, that although the controversies between the rationalists and the representatives of the Churches as to the authenticity and historical value of the Old and New Testaments and the validity of the main Christian dogmas raged continually through the last sixty years of Tennyson's life, no reference is to be found to them in his poems of this period. His

[1] I am very conscious that I may have underestimated or misinterpreted Tennyson's belief in the divinity of Christ, which probably varied from time to time. Whatever may have been his views on this point, I feel one cannot overstate his reverence for Christ's personality and teaching. Just before the publication of *In Memoriam* he is recorded as saying, with the use of an unusual word, borrowed from Sir Walter Scott, 'Christianty is rugging at my heart.'

mind had turned to more fundamental problems and was henceforward occupied with questions that admit only a metaphysical answer.

The main theme of *In Memoriam* is the possibility of a life—or continued existence of the human spirit—after human death. This was the question discussed in 'The Two Voices' from another point of view—namely the justification of suicide. The discussion in *In Memoriam* proceeds from Tennyson's intense longing for conviction that his spirit is not to be permanently severed from Arthur's, nor the beauty of Arthur's spirit and its capacity for active good wholly extinguished.

During the first twenty-nine sections, which cover the last three months of 1833, the Poet is too much crushed by his loss to be able to think of anything beyond its immediate effects. The earliest reference to the possibility of spiritual survival is in Section XXX, which describes the first Christmas spent at Somersby after Arthur's death. Here the idea flashes suddenly out with an intense gleam of hope and consolation:

> *Our voices took a higher range;*
> *Once more we sang 'They do not die*
> *Nor lose their mortal sympathy,*
> *Nor change to us, although they change; . . .'*

But this gleam of confidence is evanescent, and in Section XXXIV the poet falls back on a much more tentative statement:

> *My own dim life should teach me this,*
> *That life shall live for evermore,*
> *Else life is darkness at the core,*
> *And dust and ashes all that is;*
>
> *This round of green, this orb of flame,*
> *Fantastic beauty; such as lurks*
> *In some wild poet, when he works*
> *Without a conscience or an aim.*
>
> *What then were God to such as I?*
> *'Twere hardly worth my while to choose*
> *Of things all mortal, or to use*
> *A little patience ere I die;*

The question thus links itself in his mind with still more fundamental problems—for example, that of the Divine guidance of the universe.

LIV

*Oh yet we trust that somehow good*
*Will be the final goal of ill,*
*To pangs of nature, sins of will,*
*Defects of doubt, and taints of blood;*

*That nothing walks with aimless feet;*
*That not one life shall be destroy'd,*
*Or cast as rubbish to the void,*
*When God hath made the pile complete;*

*That not a worm is cloven in vain;*
*That not a moth with vain desire*
*Is shrivell'd in a fruitless fire,*
*Or but subserves another's gain.*

*Behold, we know not anything;*
*I can but trust that good shall fall*
*At last—far off—at last, to all,*
*And every winter change to spring.*

*So runs my dream: but what am I?*
*An infant crying in the night:*
*An infant crying for the light:*
*And with no language but a cry.*

His doubts are reinforced by the results of recent discoveries in natural science, such as the biological work of Cuvier and Charles Lyell's *Principles of Geology*, which he had studied closely.

The cruelty and wastefulness of Nature seem wholly inconsistent with the idea of a beneficent Creator and of love as the all-pervading law of the universe.

LV

*Are God and Nature then at strife*
*That Nature lends such evil dreams?*
*So careful of the type she seems,*
*So careless of the single life;*

*That I, considering everywhere*
*Her secret meaning in her deeds,*
*And finding that of fifty seeds*
*She often brings but one to bear,*

*I falter where I firmly trod,*
*And falling with my weight of cares*
*Upon the great world's altar-stairs*
*That slope thro' darkness up to God,*

*I stretch lame hands of faith, and grope,*
*And gather dust and chaff, and call*
*To what I feel is Lord of all,*
*And faintly trust the larger hope.*

LVI

*'So careful of the type?' but no,*
*From scarped cliff and quarried stone*
*She cries, 'A thousand types are gone;*
*I care for nothing, all shall go.*

*Thou makest thine appeal to me:*
*I bring to life, I bring to death:*
*The spirit does but mean the breath:*
*I know no more.' And he, shall he,*

*Man, her last work, who seem'd so fair,*
*Such splendid purpose in his eyes,*
*Who roll'd the psalm to wintry skies,*
*Who built him fanes of fruitless prayer,*

*Who trusted God was love indeed*
*And love Creation's final law—*
*Tho' Nature, red in tooth and claw*
*With ravine, shriek'd against his creed—*

*Who loved, who suffer'd countless ills,*
*Who battled for the True, the Just,*
*Be blown about the desert dust,*
*Or seal'd within the iron hills?*

*No more? A monster then, a dream,*
*A discord. Dragons of the prime,*
*That tare each other in their slime,*
*Were mellow music match'd with him.*

*O life as futile, then, as frail!*
*O for thy voice to soothe and bless!*
*What hope of answer, or redress?*
*Behind the veil, behind the veil.*

This phase of Tennyson's mental struggle may be placed in the year succeeding Arthur's death (1834), for the sections depicting it come between Section XXX, which describes the Christmas of 1833, and Section LXXVIII, which describes that of the succeeding year. As the violence of grief abates, the poem is marked by a gradually increasing serenity. The poet is able to dwell more calmly on memories of his friendship and on the thought of what Arthur would have become had he lived. He even discusses the possibility that Arthur's spirit may be revealed to him in life. Then, in Section XCV, he is visited by one of those mystical experiences which I have described. Sitting in the garden at Somersby one night, after all the household have gone to bed, he reads over Arthur's letters:

*And strangely on the silence broke*
*The silent-speaking words, and strange*
*Was love's dumb cry defying change*
*To test his worth: and strangely spoke*

*The faith, the vigour, bold to dwell*
*On doubts that drive the coward back,*
*And keen thro' wordy snares to track*
*Suggestion to her inmost cell.*

*So word by word, and line by line,*
*The dead man touch'd me from the past,*
*And all at once it seem'd at last*
*The living soul was flash'd on mine,*

*And mine in this was wound, and whirl'd*
*About empyreal heights of thought,*
*And came on that which is, and caught*
*The deep pulsations of the world,*

*Aeonian music measuring out*
*The steps of Time—the shocks of Chance—*
*The blows of Death. At length my trance*
*Was cancell'd, stricken thro' with doubt.*

*Vague words! but ah, how hard to frame*
*In matter-moulded forms of speech,*
*Or ev'n for intellect to reach*
*Thro' memory that which I became:*

*Till now the doubtful dusk reveal'd*
*The knolls once more where, couch'd at ease,*
*The white kine glimmer'd, and the trees*
*Laid their dark arms about the field:*

*And suck'd from out the distant gloom*
*A breeze began to tremble o'er*
*The large leaves of the sycamore,*
*And fluctuate all the still perfume,*

*And gathering freshlier overhead,*
*Rock'd the full-foliaged elms, and swung*
*The heavy-folded rose, and flung*
*The lilies to and fro, and said*

*'The dawn, the dawn,' and died away;*
*And East and West, without a breath,*
*Mixt their dim lights, like life and death,*
*To broaden into boundless day.*

It is characteristic of Tennyson's love of truth, and evidence of the genuineness of this experience, that in the original version the end of the third stanza and beginning of the fourth ran as follows:

His *living soul was flash'd on mine,*
*And mine in* his *was wound. . . .*

Looking back over the years, Tennyson felt unable to say with certainty that it was Arthur's spirit with which he established communication. He therefore substituted the more general description, quoted above.

With the family's removal from Somersby to Epping (Sections C to CIII), which brought Tennyson nearer to his friends and the active pulse of life in London, a fresh hopefulness is apparent, and in the famous New Year section, 'Ring out, wild bells', he reverts once more to his old dream of the moral evolution of man (hinted at in earlier poems, such as 'The Poet's Song', 'The Sleeping Beauty' ['L'Envoi'], 'Locksley Hall' and *The Princess*, Canto VII), and the coming of a purer and truer Christianity.

*Ring out the darkness of the land,*
*Ring in the Christ that is to be.*

This idea was to receive an exciting stimulus from the theory of biological evolution, which, as I have said above, was first clearly enunciated by R. W. Chambers in his *Vestiges of the Natural History of Creation* (1844), fifteen years before Darwin seemed to complete its establishment by his theory of Natural Selection. Tennyson, who had divined the possibility of the evolution of species from his study of Cuvier while at Cambridge (see *Alfred Tennyson*, p. 83), clearly refers to it in Section CXVIII:

*. . . . They say,*
*The solid earth whereon we tread*

*In tracts of fluent heat began,*
*And grew to seeming random forms,*
*The seeming prey of cyclic storms,*
*Till at the last arose the man;*

*Who throve and branch'd from clime to clime,*
*The herald of a higher race,*
*And of himself in higher place,*
*If so he type this work of time*

*Within himself, from more to more;*

But it is not until Section CXXI that the conclusions of the poem begin to appear, tentatively at first, but with growing confidence, also with an entirely new and much broader conception of the possible meaning of spiritual survival.

In CXXIV Tennyson is able to affirm unmistakably his belief in a divine and fatherly guidance of the universe, though he can still only base this relief on the 'heat of inward evidence' referred to in 'The Two Voices':

*A warmth within the breast would melt*
*The freezing reason's colder part,*
*And like a man in wrath the heart*
*Stood up and answer'd 'I have felt.'*

In CXXVI he reaffirms his conviction that God is Love and Love the guiding force of the Universe. In CXXII he hints at an idea which he had first touched on in 'Oenone': that the function of man's free will is so to attune itself to the divine law that ultimately:

*the full grown will*
*Circled thro' all experiences, pure law,*
*Commeasure perfect freedom.*

This idea is also clearly and forcibly expressed in the Prefatory stanzas to *In Memoriam*, written after the rest of the poem in 1849:

*Our wills are ours, we know not how;*
*Our will are ours to make them thine.*[1]

Tennyson's acceptance of this idea of the universality of law suggests that he had been convinced by Mill and his predecessors, Spinoza and Laplace, of the validity of the law of Universal Causation. (Cf. 'Locksley Hall', 'Sixty Years After': 'Hold the Present fatal daughter of the Past'.) In Tennyson's creed, however, the law is of divine origin, and he refuses to believe that it can preclude the freedom of the human will, though he cannot explain precisely how the two principles can be reconciled. Here, again, he has to rely on the 'heat of inward evidence'. He now sees that the higher sphere, the universal and all-embracing spirit of Love, is not separate from but inclusive of the lower sphere, 'the course of human things' (CXXVIII): that human history (the 'vast eddies in the flood of onward time'), the trifling daily events in millions of human lives, the work of poets, scientists, historians, all:

*. . . as in some piece of art,*
*Is toil co-operant to an end.* (*Ib.*)

It is curious that he nowhere in *In Memoriam* mentions the idea that time as well as matter is an illusion. He had outlined this in *The Princess* three or four years before:

*For was, and is, and will be, are but is;*
*And all creation is one act at once,*
*The birth of light: but we that are not all,*
*As parts, can see but parts, now this, now that,*
*And live, perforce, from thought to thought, and make*
*One act a phantom of succession; thus*
*Our weakness somehow shapes the shadow, Time.*

[1] *Cf.* Francis Herbert Bradley, *Ethical Studies*, 1876. How can the human divine ideal ever be my will? The answer is, 'Your will it never can be as the will of your private self . . . to that self you must die and by faith be made one with that ideal. You must resolve to give up your will as the will of this or that man and you must put your whole self, your entire will, into the will of the divine.'

Forty years later he stated the same idea more briefly:

*But with the Nameless is nor Day nor Hour;*
*Tho' we, thin minds, who creep from thought to thought,*
*Break into 'Thens' and 'Whens' the Eternal Now:*
*This double seeming of the single world!*
('The Ancient Sage')

This thought would have helped greatly towards establishing his vision in *In Memoriam* of the 'double seeming of the single world', although it would have added to the difficulty of establishing the freedom of the human will.

The poet's new breadth of vision changes the nature of his belief in survival after death. He sees that personality has a different meaning in the higher sphere to that which it has in the lower, although human intelligence cannot clearly grasp the difference. Arthur is now 'known and unknown', 'human and divine', 'mix'd with God and nature', 'Loved deeplier, darklier understood', and most deeply loved when the Poet realizes the 'double seeming' of the world—that 'There is a lower and a higher'.

All these threads are gathered together in the last stanzas of the Epilogue, in which Tennyson speaks of his friend as a type of the higher man who is to result from human evolution and as a spirit, now living in God:

*That God which ever lives and loves*
*One God, one law, one element,*
*And one far-off divine event,*
*To which the whole creation moves.*

In these four lines and the last stanza of Section CXXXI are included the ideas of God as Creator, God as love, God as law, and God as will, guiding and drawing all His creation to a final divine and perfect consummation, which will involve the 'closing' of all human personalities with each other and with His divine personality, 'soul in soul'.

I think Tennyson's use of the word 'close' shows that he was not thinking of a complete absorption or merger of the human spirit in the divine, but of a relation which in some way that he could not attempt to define more clearly would leave the human spirit a degree of individuality. Later he hinted at the same conception when he described the human spirit as a ripple on the boundless deep, which

> *Feels that the deep is boundless, and itself*
> *For ever changing form, but evermore*
> *One with the boundless motion of the deep.*

After the grand sweep and confidence of the final sections of *In Memoriam*, the introductory stanzas, although no doubt written later, must seem tentative and diffident. This is inevitable. These stanzas are intended to be an introduction to the whole poem, with its doubts, confusions and contradictions, and a summary of the moods through which the Poet passed during its composition. The main themes of the poem are, however, emphasized—the divine supremacy of Love and universal law (confidently), and the immortality of the spirit (hopefully). But emphasis is laid on the relativity of all human theories and systems and on the impossibility of knowledge in subjects beyond human comprehension:

> *We have but faith. We cannot know,*
> *For Knowledge is of things we see.*[1]

So strongly did Tennyson feel this that in after life he came to doubt whether the conclusions of *In Memoriam* are not too definite and thought of adding a section to modify them. Fortunately he never carried this thought into effect.

The introductory stanzas do however suggest, in contrast to the more vague theism of the Epilogue, that the Poet had been strongly influenced by the metaphysical theology of St. John and St. Paul. It is impossible not to feel that the 'strong Son of God, immortal Love' of the opening line represents the poet's conception of Christ, otherwise it is difficult to give any satisfactory meaning to the words:

> *Thou seemest human and divine,*
> *The highest, holiest manhood, thou.*

[1] There is precedent for this distinction in Kant's theory of *Phenomena and Noumena*. Tennyson elaborated his views in 'The Ancient Sage'. (See pp. 116 and 117.)

But the second stanza:

*Thine are these orbs of light and shade;*
*Thou madest life in man and brute;*
*Thou madest Death; and lo, thy foot*
*Is on the skull which thou hast made.*

and much of the rest of the poem seem more in keeping with one's idea of God, the Father and Creator, than with the Jesus of the Gospels.

This conception of Christ is, however, quite in harmony with the theology of John and Paul. Tennyson himself, when asked as to the meaning of the words 'Immortal Love', said that they might 'be taken in a St. John sense'; and Hallam Tennyson (Annotated Edition, p. 943) refers to 'St. John, iv and v'. Evidently Tennyson had in mind, e.g., St. John's first Epistle, Ch. iv, verse 7: 'Beloved, let us love one another; for love is of God; and everyone that loveth is born of God, and knoweth God'; and verse 16: 'God is love and he that dwelleth in love dwelleth in God, and God in him.' There seems also to be a clear affinity with the first chapter of St. John's Gospel:

> In the beginning was the Word, and the Word was with God, and the Word was God. The same was in the beginning with God. All things were made by him; and without him was not anything made. . . . He was in the world, and the world was made by him, and the world knew him not.

So also in Hebrews i, 2, God is said to have 'spoken to us by his Son, whom he hath appointed his heir of all things, by whom also he made the worlds'; and in 1 Corinthians viii, 6, St. Paul says:

> There is but one God the Father, of whom are all things, and we in him: and one Lord Jesus Christ, by whom are all things and we in him.

and in Colossians i, 16, even more definitely:

> For by him [God the Son] were all things created, that are in heaven, and that are in earth, visible and invisible . . . all things were created by him and for him. . . .

an idea which is emphasized in the Nicene Creed 'By whom all things were made', while in Colossians ii, 10, Christ is spoken of as 'the head of all principality and power', and in 1 Timothy vi, 15, as 'the blessed and only Potentate the King of Kings and Lord of lords'. It seems therefore that, whatever view Tennyson may have held about the divinity of the Jesus of the Gospels, he did regard him as an incarnation or expression of the divine Love, which he believed to be the creative and guiding spirit of the universe, and that it was in this sense that he interpreted the teaching of St. John and St. Paul.

The thought of Arthur Hallam as a type of the ideal man, set out at the end of the Epilogue of *In Memoriam*, probably influenced Tennyson in the decision he made during the 1850s to attempt a work of large scope on the subject of King Arthur and the Round Table. He had, ever since his early manhood, wished to take up the Arthurian legends, which he considered the finest of all subjects for an English poet; but he never liked to handle an old story unless he could in some way give it a relevance to contemporary life and problems. The story of King Arthur's struggles to rescue his country from the Romans and the heathen and to build up an ideal polity through the formation of his Order of the Knights of the Round Table, bound to him

*. . . by such vows, as is a shame*
*A man should not be bound by, yet the which*
*No man can keep.*

seemed to Tennyson instinct with a symbolism which might be of real value to the age. 'I tried in my *Idylls* to teach men the need of the ideal,' he said thirty years later, and he made his purpose perfectly clear when he added the Epilogue *To the Queen* in 1872, for he then described the *Idylls of the King* as an

*. . . old, imperfect tale,*
*New-old and shadowing Sense at war with Soul,*
*Rather than that gray King, whose name, a ghost,*
*Streams like a cloud, manshaped, from mountain peak,*
*And cleaves to cairn and cromlech still.*

Tennyson much disliked being too strictly pinned down in the interpretation of his poems, and he would certainly have disliked the attempts which some writers have made to attach precise symbolical meanings to the various characters and incidents of the *Idylls.*[1] It is enough for our present purpose to say that Arthur, in Tennyson's scheme, represents the ideal or spiritual principle trying to realize itself in the world of sense (through marriage with Guinevere). Lancelot may perhaps be taken as an embodiment of the poetic spirit which should be the chief support and interpreter of the spiritual (Lancelot was Arthur's chief Knight and sent by him to fetch Guinevere for their marriage), and Merlin seems to embody the rationalistic and scientific intellect. When the poetic spirit is overcome by the sensual and science succumbs to the lure of materialism, fatal blows are struck at the Quest for the Ideal, the inevitable failure and undying persistence of which are symbolized by the defeat of Arthur and his promised return from Avalon, while the relativity of even the noblest human embodiments of the ideal is implied in the famous lines of 'Morte d'Arthur':

> *The old order changeth, yielding place to new,*
> *And God fulfils himself in many ways,*
> *Lest one good custom should corrupt the world.*

The *Idylls* is essentially a religious poem (the Lady of the Lake, who takes especial care of Arthur and is described as the mystic foster-mother of Lancelot, undoubtedly typifies the Christian Religion) and the whole poem is deeply charged with Christian feeling and symbolism. The nature of the subject, however, with its romantic mediaevalism, and Tennyson's dramatic method of treatment, are such that the poem, while it emphasizes the poet's deep sense of the moral beauty of 'the Creed of Creeds', can add little to our knowledge of his philosophical interpretation of it. From the latter point of view the most important episode in the whole collection of stories is 'The Holy Grail'. The Grail obviously represents the extreme mystical approach to religion.

[1] The characters in the *Idylls* are what Miss Dorothy Sayers, in an interesting discussion of the symbolism of the *Divine Comedy*, has described as 'natural symbols'. It is not the conventional symbolism where a stout lady with a flaming torch represents war and an equally stout lady with an olive wreath or dove, peace. The vices and virtues of the personalities described and the events which result from these naturally represent the larger movements symbolized.

Tennyson was at heart a mystic with a capacity for true mystical experience, and many critics have thought it strange that he should have made the Quest of the Grail one of the principal causes of the collapse of Arthur's scheme and depicted Arthur himself as so unfriendly to the Quest. This attitude illustrates Tennyson's deep-seated conviction that the highest life is 'with man and for man', a conviction which is illustrated from a different angle by the conclusion of 'Sixty Years After'. He saw that for the ordinary mind to turn away from the ordinary duties of human society in order deliberately to seek mystical experience, or deliberately cultivate religious exaltation, is dangerous and almost certain to be injurious, although for the exceptional spirit, like Galahad or Perceval's sister, the Holy Nun, the effort may be fruitful. Tennyson's view on this subject is expressed in the speech with which Arthur, who was absent when the Grail vision first appeared in the Hall at Camelot, sums up the results of the Quest:

*'And spake I not too truly, O my knights?*
*Was I too dark a prophet when I said*
*To those who went upon the Holy Quest,*
*That most of them would follow wandering fires*
*Lost in the quagmire?—lost to me and gone,*
*And left me gazing at a barren board,*
*And a lean Order—scarce return'd a tithe—*
*And out of those to whom the vision came*
*My greatest hardly will believe he saw;*
*Another hath beheld it afar off,*
*And leaving human wrongs to right themselves,*
*Cares but to pass into the silent life.*
*And one hath had the vision face to face,*
*And now his chair desires him here in vain,*
*However they may crown him otherwhere.*

*'And some among you held, that if the King*
*Had seen the sight he would have sworn the vow;*
*Not easily, seeing that the King must guard*
*That which he rules, and is but as the hind*
*To whom a space of land is given to plow.*
*Who may not wander from the allotted field*

*Before his work be done; but, being done,*
*Let visions of the night or of the day*
*Come, as they will; and many a time they come,*
*Until this earth he walks on seems not earth,*
*This light that strikes his eyeball is not light,*
*This air that smites his forehead is not air*
*But vision—yea, his very hand and foot—*
*In moments when he feels he cannot die,*
*And knows himself no vision to himself,*
*Nor the high God a vision, nor that One*
*Who rose again: ye have seen what ye have seen.'*

After the completion of the *Idylls of the King*, Tennyson devoted the greater part of ten years to the drama. For his three most important plays he chose subjects illustrating the age-long struggle between England and the Papacy—Harold, Becket and Queen Mary. But although the choice of subject may have been influenced by the strong feeling which had been aroused in England during the 'sixties and early 'seventies by the aggressive policy of Rome, culminating in the confirmation by the Oecumenical Council of 1871 of the dogma of Papal infallibility, Tennyson treated his theme in these three plays from a political rather than a religious point of view. His sympathies were, of course, with the Protestant cause, but he had long ago lost interest in dogma of all kinds, and his attitude to doctrinal controversy is shown in the brief scene outside Queen Mary's death chamber which I have quoted on p. 59.

Tennyson's concentration on the historical drama did not, however, weaken his interest in the movement of contemporary thought. While working on his plays he maintained a considerable lyric output, and continued, in a number of poems, to discuss from varying points of view the great religious questions, his earlier reactions to which I have already tried to describe. His attitude during these later years was strongly influenced by the rapid advance of rationalistic thought. In 1855 there had appeared two very important works, Alexander Bain's *Senses and Intellect* and Spencer's *Principles of Psychology*. Bain analysed all mental operations, whether human or animal, into sensory and motor experiences, entirely dependent on nervous structure and function; maintained that the animal mind differs from the human mind not in kind but only in degree, and suggested that it was impossible to divorce will or mind from their biological conditions or material environment. Spencer reached very much the same conclusions by different methods. He claimed that all knowledge comes from experience and has no other conceivable source. Experience, however, he suggested, is of two kinds: the direct experience of the individual and the accumulated experience of the race, organized in the brain by a process of gradual deposition and accretion and transmitted through successive generations. The arguments of both philosophers supported the view that our volitions are completely determined, being the inevitable consequences of chains of cause and effect. Both seriously challenged man's claim to free will and to any continued existence after death. In 1859 came Darwin's *Origin of Species*, attributing the development of the various species of living creatures on the earth entirely to adaptations forced on them by the struggle for existence. Buckle, in the first volume of his *Introduction to a History of Civilization in England* (1857), followed up the views of Bain and Spencer and obtained for them a much wider hearing, as he wrote with greater popular appeal. In 1860 there appeared in the *Westminster Review* an article entitled 'Neo-Christianity', in which Frederic Harrison, a young Oxford Positivist, violently attacked the Broad Church movement, of which Tennyson's friends F. D. Maurice and Benjamin Jowett were leaders, and prophesied that this would not save Christianity from collapse. Comte's influence was meanwhile growing rapidly on the Continent and in England, where rationalists welcomed his contention that theology and metaphysics must both be displaced by science and the future progress of society entirely guided by a scientific view based on the positive data of experience. Tennyson particularly disliked Comte's philosophy, not least his *Religion of Humanity*, which was to be unique as having no supernatural or non-natural articles of belief—'Catholicism without Christianity' as it was called by one of its critics. Spencer's synthetic philosophy with its mechanistic basis was a similar and increasing influence.

In 1867, Swinburne's *Poems and Ballads* raised the banner of poetic revolt on behalf of an essentially amoral pagan rationalism, and his *Songs before Sunrise*, which followed in 1871, have been described by J. B. Bury as 'a seedplot of atheism and revolution, sown with implacable hatred of creeds and tyrants'. In the following year appeared Winwood Reade's *Martyrdom of Man*, a rationalistic survey of man's history, the results of which the author summed up as follows:

> Supernatural Christianity is false. God-worship is idolatry. Prayer is useless. The soul is not immortal. There are no rewards and there are no punishments in a future state.

Tennyson knew and liked Reade, and this book affected him powerfully.

1874 marked the high-water mark of the rationalistic tide. In that year Tyndall, another close friend of Tennyson, delivered his famous Belfast address before the British Association. In this he claimed to 'wrest from theology the entire domain of cosmological theory', and said that he could 'discern in matter the promise and potency of all terrestrial life'. Before the same meeting Huxley read a paper on *Animal Automatism*, in which he maintained that our so-called voluntary movements are not the effect of our volitions, but of certain molecular changes in the nervous system by which those volitions are accompanied, so that consciousness has in fact no power over our actions. In December, W. K. Clifford printed in the *Fortnightly Review* a paper on 'Body and Mind', in which he argued against 'the possible existence of consciousness apart from a nervous system, of mind without body'—and said that 'a revival of any form of sacerdotal Christianity would be an appalling calamity for the human race'.

When one adds to these outstanding statements the work of John Morley, Leslie Stephen, John Holyoake and Charles Bradlaugh, it becomes clear how great was the growth of the Rationalist movement during the forty years that succeeded the publication of *In Memoriam*.

Tennyson's reaction to these tendencies took two forms: direct or thinly veiled counter-attack and positive statement of his own creed.

In the former class comes 'Despair', first published in 1881. The speaker of this wild monologue is a man who has been rescued from attempted suicide, to which he has been driven by his loss of belief in God. He has been brought up in a fatalistic Calvinist creed,[1] Tennyson's description of which suggests a reminiscent horror of the hell-fire doctrines of his aunt Mary Bourne, and has abandoned it because he could not accept a creed which involved a belief in eternal punishment. Unfortunately, he does not turn to a true religion of love, but is misled by the 'know-nothing books' of contemporary rationalists into atheism.

V

*Hoped for a dawn and it came, but the promise had faded away;*
*We had passed from a cheerless night to the glare of a drearier day;*
*He is only a cloud and a smoke who was once a pillar of fire,*
*The guess of a worm in the dust and the shadow of its desire—*
*Of a worm as it writhes in a world of the weak trodden down by the strong,*
*Of a dying worm in a world, all massacre, murder, and wrong.*

VI

*O we poor orphans of nothing—alone on that lonely shore—*
*Born of the brainless Nature who knew not that which she bore!*
*Trusting no longer that earthly flower would be heavenly fruit—*
*Come from the brute, poor souls—no souls—and to die with the brute—*

Such a creed, which seemed to Tennyson the logical outcome of the Rationalist doctrines, could give man no reason for wishing to live.

In 1886 Tennyson published a volume which contained two important works: 'Locksley Hall, Sixty Years After' and 'The Promise of May', a drama of contemporary life, which, when put on the stage four years before, had aroused the violent hostility of the advocates of free thought, who considered it a travesty of their methods and objects. At an early performance, Lord Queensberry rose in the stalls and made a speech of violent protest, and the play had to be withdrawn after a run of only a few weeks. 'The Promise of May' tells the story of a cynical and hedonistic atheist, Philip Edgar, who seduces the daughter of a Lincolnshire farmer and then deserts her. Edgar has been convinced by the

[1] In 'Rizpah', Stanza xv, *Works*, p. 503, Tennyson had another tilt at the Calvinists. 'Election, Election and Reprobation', etc.

writings of Huxley, J. S. Mill and Alexander Bain that man is actuated entirely by a series of automatic sensations without any independent will-power. If this is true, he says, what can we do but live for pleasant sensations? Once, when man could believe in a life after death, he was willing to endure unpleasant sensations in the hope of experiencing pleasant ones after death. Now our only expectation after death is of night and silence. Nor need we shrink from pleasure for fear of inflicting pain on others. The gods are only shadows of ourselves. Nature knows nothing. Pain is inherent in Nature; so we need not worry if our pleasure causes pain to others. We must not strain to make ourselves better than Nature. Government, religion, social conventions like marriage, are all restraints upon Nature. The new democracy—Socialism, Communism, Nihilism, whatever it may be called—will sweep all these restraints away; vice and virtue are but masks of the self, and the vice of one age is the virtue of the next. Edgar acts on these principles until Fate forces him to realize something of the misery which he is causing to others, and he begins to experience a feeling of remorse wholly inconsistent with the theories of life which he has hitherto accepted.

*. . . O my God, if man be only*
*A willy-nilly current of sensations—*
*Reaction needs must follow revel—yet—*
*Why feel remorse, he, knowing that he* must *have*
*Moved in the iron grooves of Destiny?*
*Remorse then is a part of Destiny,*
*Nature a liar, making us feel guilty*
*Of her own faults.*

. . . . .

*O this mortal house,*
*Which we are born into, is haunted by*
*The ghosts of the dead passions of dead men;*
*And these take flesh again with our own flesh,*
*And bring us to confusion.*
*He was only*
*A poor philosopher who call'd the mind*
*Of children a blank page, a* tabula rasa.
*There, there, is written in invisible inks*

> *'Lust, Prodigality, Covetousness, Craft,*
> *Cowardice, Murder'—and the heat and fire*
> *Of life will bring them out, and black enough,*
> *So the child grow to manhood: better death*
> *With our first wail than life—*

Edgar now finds himself wondering:

> *When man has surely learnt at last that all*
> *His old world faith, the blossom of his youth,*
> *Has faded, falling fruitless—whether then*
> *All of us, all at once, may not be seized*
> *With some fierce passion, not so much for Death*
> *As against life! All, all, into the dark—*
> *No more!—and science now could drug and balm us*
> *Back into nescience with as little pain*
> *As if to fall asleep.*

In the end he finds, when it is too late, that he has destroyed his own happiness as well as that of his victims.

In 'Locksley Hall, Sixty Years After', Tennyson again attacked with extraordinary violence the blend of democratic Socialism, amorality and free thought which the Rationalists were propagating. He felt that these were eating away the old idealism, which he considered to be essential for human progress.

The poem shows the hero of the first 'Locksley Hall', now an old man of eighty, coming back, in a mood of reconciliation and forgiveness, to the Hall for the funeral of his former rival, who has died after a long life of unobtrusive usefulness as Squire and landlord.

Through the old man's soliloquy Tennyson undoubtedly sublimated much of his own life experience—the family quarrels that had embittered his youth, the frustration of his first love for Rosa Baring (which I am now inclined to think was a more serious blow to him than I had previously imagined), the deep consolation and happiness of his marriage with Emily Sellwood, the shock of his son Lionel's early death, his growing sense of isolation through the loss of so many devoted friends of his youth, and, parallel with all this, the movement of his own beliefs and hopes since the composition of the first poem in the late 1830s.

He stresses again the essential need of pursuing the ideal without regard for consequences and the indispensability of a belief in the immortality of the human spirit

*Truth for Truth, and good for good! The Good, the True, the Pure, the Just—*
*Take the charm 'For ever' from them, and they crumble into dust.*

Looking back he feels that the belief in the perfectibility of man, which had been fostered by the scientific and political developments of the first part of the century, has been cruelly falsified.

*Gone the cry of 'Forward, Forward' lost within a growing gloom;*
*Lost, or only heard in silence from the silence of a tomb.*

*Half the marvels of my morning, triumphs over time and space,*
*Staled by frequence, shrunk by usage into commonest commonplace!*

There seems actually to have been a deterioration rather than an improvement in the social conscience.

*Is it well that while we range with Science, glorying in the Time,*
*City children soak and blacken soul and sense in city slime?*

*There among the glooming alleys Progress halts on palsied feet,*
*Crime and hunger cast our maidens by the thousand on the street.*

*There the Master scrimps his haggard sempstress of her daily bread,*
*There a single sordid attic holds the living and the dead.*

*There the smouldering fire of fever creeps across the rotted floor,*
*And the crowded couch of incest in the warrens of the poor.*

The agrarian outrages in Ireland, the dynamite and revolvers of Fenians and Anarchists, make him feel that the modern world, far from progressing during the first half of the century, has fallen below 'the passions of the primal clan'. Greatest folly of all has been the reckless extension of the Franchise—now almost manhood suffrage—in a country where only a minute fraction of the people had any appreciable education and the educated classes were losing the idealism and sincerity needed for true guidance. How could such an Electorate deal with vast problems like that of India with her 300 millions of people, and the menace of Russia on her northern frontiers?

*Russia bursts our Indian barrier, shall we fight her? shall we yield?*
*Pause! before you sound the trumpet, hear the voices from the field.*

*Those three hundred millions under one Imperial sceptre now,*
*Shall we hold them? shall we loose them? take the suffrage of the plow.*[1]

*Nay, but these would feel and follow Truth if only you and you,*
*Rivals of realm-ruining party, when you speak were wholly true.*

*Plowmen, Shepherds, have I found, and more than once, and still could find*
*Sons of God, and kings of men in utter nobleness of mind,*

*Truthful, trustful, looking upward to the practised hustings-liar;*
*So the Higher wields the Lower, while the Lower is the Higher.*

*Here and there a cottar's babe is royal-born by right divine;*
*Here and there my Lord is lower than his oxen or his swine.*

*Chaos, Cosmos! Cosmos, Chaos! once again the sickening game;*
*Freedom, free to slay herself, and dying while they shout her name.*

*Step by step we gain'd a freedom known to Europe, known to all;*
*Step by step we rose to greatness–thro' the tonguesters we may fall.*

*You that woo the Voices—tell them 'old experience is a fool',*
*Teach your flatter'd kings that only those who cannot read can rule.*

*Pluck the mighty from their seat, but set no meek ones in their place;*
*Pillory Wisdom in your markets, pelt your offal at her face.*

*Tumble Nature heel o'er head, and, yelling with the yelling street,*
*Set the feet above the brain and swear the brain is in the feet.*

*Bring the old dark ages back without the faith, without the hope,*
*Break the State, the Church, the Throne, and roll their ruins down the slope.*

*Authors—essayist, atheist, novelist, realist, rhymester, play your part,*
*Paint the mortal shame of nature with the living hues of Art.*

*Rip your brothers' vices open, strip your own foul passions bare;*
*Down with Reticence, down with Reverence—forward—naked—let them stare.*

[1] Perhaps a reference to Gladstone's Franchise Act. (See above, p. 64.)

*Feed the budding rose of boyhood with the drainage of your sewer;*
*Send the drain into the fountain, lest the stream should issue pure.*

*Set the maiden fancies wallowing in the troughs of Zolaism—*
*Forward, forward, ay and backward, downward too into the abysm.*

*Do your best to charm the worst, to lower the rising race of men;*
*Have we risen from out the beast, then back into the beast again?*

*Only 'dust to dust' for me that sicken at your lawless din,*
*Dust in wholesome old-world dust before the newer world begin.*

Yet the old man will not altogether give up the hopes of his youth: some day, perhaps in the infinitely distant future, the anarchist's dream may be realized.

*Ay, for doubtless I am old, and think gray thoughts, for I am gray:*
*After all the stormy changes shall we find a changeless May?*

*After madness, after massacre, Jacobinism and Jacquerie,*
*Some diviner force to guide us thro' the days I shall not see?*

*When the schemes and all the systems, Kingdoms and Republics fall,*
*Something kindlier, higher, holier—all for each and each for all?*

*All the full brain, half brain races, led by Justice, Love and Truth;*
*All the millions one at length with all the visions of my youth?*

*All diseases quenched by Science, no man halt, or deaf or blind;*
*Stronger ever born of weaker, lustier body, larger mind?*

*Earth at last a warless world, a single race, a single tongue—*
*I have seen her far away—for is not Earth as yet so young?*

*Every tiger madness muzzled, every serpent passion kill'd,*
*Every grim ravine a garden, every blazing desert till'd,*

*Robed in universal harvest up to either pole she smiles,*
*Universal ocean softly washing all her warless Isles.*

But if Malthus was right in his view that population inevitably tends to increase faster than the means of subsistence, how can one really hope that such dreams will be realized, and war eliminated?

> *Warless? war will die out late then will it ever? late or soon?*
> *Can it, till this outworn earth be dead, as yon dead world the moon?*

Our limited knowledge cannot provide an answer. After all, our Earth is but an insignificant part of the Universe, of the rest of which we know almost nothing, and these apparently destructive movements are only eddies in a vast ocean, the movements of which our finite minds cannot possibly grasp. The new astronomy may call the moon dead:

*Dead, but how her living glory lights the hall, the dune, the grass!*
*Yet the moonlight is the sunlight, and the sun himself will pass.*

*Venus near her! smiling downward at this earthlier earth of ours,*
*Closer on the sun, perhaps a world of never fading flowers.*

*Hesper, whom the poet call'd the Bringer home of all good things.*
*All good things may move in Hesper, perfect peoples, perfect kings.*

*Hesper—Venus—were we natives to that splendour or in Mars,*
*We should see the Globe we groan in, fairest of their evening stars.*

*Could we dream of wars and carnage, craft and madness, lust and spite,*
*Roaring London, raving Paris, in that point of peaceful light?*

*Might we not in glancing heavenward on a star so silver-fair,*
*Yearn, and clasp the hands and murmur, 'Would to God that we were there.'*

*Forward, backward, backward, forward, in the immeasurable sea,*
*Sway'd by vaster ebbs and flows than can be known to you or me.*

*All the suns—are these but symbols of innumerable man,*
*Man or Mind that sees a shadow of the planner or the plan?*

*Is there evil but on earth? or pain in every peopled sphere?*
*Well be grateful for the sounding watchword 'Evolution' here,*

*Evolution ever climbing after some ideal good,*
*And Reversion ever dragging Evolution in the mud.*

*What are men that He should heed us? cried the king of sacred song;*
*Insects of an hour, that hourly work, their brother insect wrong,*

*While the silent Heavens roll, and Suns along their fiery way,*
*All their planets whirling round them, flash a million miles a day.*

*Many an Aeon moulded earth before her highest, man, was born,*
*Many an Aeon too may pass when earth is manless and forlorn,*

*Earth so huge, and yet so bounded—pools of salt, and plots of land—*
*Shallow skin of green and azure—chains of mountain, grains of sand!*

*Only That which made us, meant us to be mightier by and by,*
*Set the sphere of all the boundless Heavens within the human eye,*

*Sent the shadow of Himself, the boundless, thro' the human soul;*
*Boundless inward, in the atom, boundless outward, in the Whole.*

. . . . .

*Nay, your pardon, cry your 'forward', yours are hope and youth, but I—*
*Eighty winters leave the dog too lame to follow with the cry,*

*Lame and old, and past his time, and passing now into the night;*
*Yet I would the rising race were half as eager for the light.*

*Light the fading gleam of Even? light the glimmer of the dawn?*
*Aged eyes may take the growing glimmer for the gleam withdrawn.*

*Far away beyond her myriad coming changes earth will be*
*Something other than the wildest modern guess of you and me.*

*Earth may reach her earthly-worst, or if she gain her earthly-best,*
*Would she find her human offspring this ideal man at rest?*

*Forward then, but still remember how the course of Time will swerve,*
*Crook and turn upon itself in many a backward streaming curve.*

Before Earth can 'gain her heavenly best' he concludes 'a God must mingle with the game'.

*Nay, there may be those about us whom we neither see nor name,*

*Felt within us as ourselves, the Powers of Good, the Powers of Ill,*
*Strowing balm, or shedding poison in the fountains of the Will.*

*Follow you the Star that lights a desert pathway, yours or mine,*
*Forward, till you see the highest Human Nature is divine.*

*Follow Light, and do the Right—for man can half-control his doom—*
*Till you find the deathless Angel seated in the vacant tomb.*

*Forward, let the stormy moment fly and mingle with the Past.*
*I that loathed have come to love him. Love will conquer at the last.*

The pessimism of 'Locksley Hall, Sixty Years After' and the

rather desperate clinging to 'the larger hope' are, no doubt, partly dramatic, in keeping with the character of the old hero, who at the beginning of the poem says of himself with palpable inaccuracy:

*Gone the fires of youth, the follies, furies, curses, passionate tears,*
*Gone like fires and floods and earthquakes of the planet's dawning years.*

But both 'Sixty Years After' and 'The Promise of May' did undoubtedly represent very strong feelings which Tennyson held with deep sincerity.

Yet in spite of the violence of these polemical poems, his own convictions were all the time gaining a new serenity, based on a now firmly established assurance of the spiritual unity of this 'double seeming single world', of which the spiritual embodiment is the only true reality. These views he would express in conversation, with a naïve earnestness which was curiously impressive. In 1865, talking to Gladstone and Dr. Symonds, he said:

'I cannot form the least notion of a brick. I don't know what it is. It is no good talking to me about atoms, extension, colour, weight—I can't penetrate the brick. But I have more distinct ideas of God, of love and such emotions, I can sympathize with God in my poor way.'

And four years later, after reading the closing lines of 'The Holy Grail' aloud to some friends, he said, with an earnestness of conviction that amazed his hearers:

'Yes, it is true; there are moments when the flesh is nothing to me, when I feel and know the flesh to be vision, God and the spiritual the only real and true. Depend upon it, the spiritual is the real: it belongs to one more than the hand and the foot. . . . You may tell me that my hand and my foot are only imaginary symbols of my existence and I could believe you; but you never, never can convince me that the *I* is not an eternal reality and that the spiritual is not the only true and real part of me.'

These beliefs he condensed as early as 1869 in 'The Higher Pantheism',[1] written for the first meeting of the Metaphysical

[1] The best metaphysical analysis of this rather difficult poem is in *The Mind of Tennyson* (1900), by E. H. Sneath, Professor of Philosophy in Yale University, an introduction to which I owe to my friend, Dr. Christine Fall, of Baylor University, Texas.

Society, which had been formed at his instigation, with a most distinguished and comprehensive membership, 'for the purpose of submitting to searching criticism the intellectual foundations of the spreading positivism and agnosticism'. In this poem he suggests that the material world, including man's physical body, is only a distorted vision or dream of the real world, which is God and which the limited senses of man can only partially perceive. The vision is therefore a sign or symbol of man's temporary division from God. God, he suggests, is 'all but that which has power to feel "I am I"'—includes, that is to say, everything except the fully developed self-conscious spiritual personalities of men—and perhaps other beings which may attain to such development. Such temporarily separate personalities will, according to the conclusion of the final sections of *In Memoriam*, ultimately 'close with' the personality of God. I think Tennyson called his poem 'The *Higher* Pantheism' because by separating the finite personality of man from the infinite personality of God it made possible the conception of a divine guidance of the finite by the infinite ('the vision of him who *reigns*') and a moral relation, founded on Love and some degree of free will, between God and man—ideas quite impossible for a normal Pantheistic philosophy.

The same idea of the unreality of the material appears in other late poems of Tennyson's. 'The Sisters', a dull poem of 1880, suddenly comes to life in four lines which betray the poet's intense feeling on the subject:

*My God, I would not live*
*Save that I think this gross hard-seeming world*
*Is our mis-shaping vision of the Powers*
*Behind the world, which make our griefs our gains.*

So, too, 'Happy', one of the most unreal of the later Ballads, has three startlingly effective stanzas in which the leper's wife contrasts the reality of spiritual love with the impermanence of its physical counterpart.

VIII

*I loved you first when young and fair, but now I love you most;*
*The fairest flesh at last is filth on which the worm will feast;*
*This poor rib-grated dungeon of the holy human ghost,*
*This house with all its hateful needs no cleaner than the beast.*

IX

*This coarse diseaseful creature which in Eden was divine,*
*This Satan-haunted ruin, this little city of sewers,*
*This wall of solid flesh that comes between your soul and mine,*
*Will vanish and give place to the beauty that endures,*

X

*The beauty that endures on the Spiritual height,*
*When we shall stand transfigured, like Christ on Hermon hill,*
*And moving each to music, soul in soul and light in light,*
*Shall flash thro' one another in a moment as we will.*

At one time Tennyson thought there might be a possibility of obtaining proof of the co-existence of the spiritual world by means of the psychic phenomena which excited an increasing amount of interest during the second half of the century. He was one of the founders of the Society for Psychical Research, in 1882, and several references to telepathic experience and psychic dreams occur in his later poems, e.g. 'Enoch Arden', 'Aylmers Field', 'The Wreck', 'Demeter', 'The Children's Hospital', while in 1889 he published 'The Ring', a poem on an intensely psychic theme, which contained a definite statement of belief:

*The ghost in man, the ghost that once was man*
*But cannot wholly free itself from Man,*
*Are calling to each other thro' a dawn*
*Stranger than earth has ever seen; the veil*
*Is rending, and the Voices of the day*
*Are heard across the Voices of the dark.*

There is no parallel to this in any other of his works, nor, so far as I know, in any recorded conversation. Indeed, he was apt to be rather scathing about the performances of mediums and *séances*. Perhaps, therefore, the statement should be considered largely dramatic.

Tennyson found stronger support for his belief in the unreality of the material and the reality of the spiritual world in the mystics' power of spiritual communion and the capacity of the human mind to transcend the material and in some sense apprehend infinity, thereby showing its kinship with the Infinite. In 'The Voice and the Peak' he writes:

*The Peak is high and flush'd*
*At its highest with sunrise fire:*
*The Peak is high and the stars are high*
*And the thought of a man is higher.*

With which one can compare the lines already quoted from 'Locksley Hall, Sixty Years After':

*. . . That which made us, meant us to be mightier by and by,*
*Set the sphere of all the boundless Heavens within the human eye,*

*Sent the shadow of Himself, the boundless, thro' the human soul;*
*Boundless inward, in the atom, boundless outward, in the Whole.*

He still finds it necessary to stress again and again that belief in spiritual survival ('the cardinal point of Christianity' he called it) is essential if human life is to have any meaning, and these later affirmations sometimes revert to the more primitive type of statement which was characteristic of the earlier sections of *In Memoriam*: see 'Despair', Stanzas XIII and XIV and the lines already quoted from 'Locksley Hall, Sixty Years After' (above, p. 103):

*Truth for Truth, and Good for Good!*[1] *The Good, the True, the Pure, the Just,*
*Take the charm 'for ever' from them and they crumble into dust.*

By 'Truth for Truth', etc., I think Tennyson meant that man should pursue truth and virtue for their own sakes and not in the hope of future reward, but that unless the human spirit is to survive, such a pursuit becomes meaningless, because the result of it is annihilated. So, too, in the Epilogue to *Tiresias* and 'A Voice Spake out of the Skies'. In 'Wages' he makes it clear that this insistence on a belief in spiritual survival is not due to the need of a reward to make well-doing worth while, but solely because of

[1] Cf. 'Oenone':

*And because right is right, to follow right*
*Were wisdom in the scorn of consequence.*

the wanton waste which the annihilation of the spiritual in man would involve.[1]

*The wages of sin is death: if the wages of Virtue be dust,*
*Would she have heart to endure for the life of the worm and the fly?*
*She desires no isles of the blest, no quiet seats of the just,*
*To rest in a golden grove, or to bask in a summer sky:*
*Give her the wages of going on, and not to die.*[2]

And he repeated the same idea in 'Vastness' (1889), where he also based his belief on his conviction of the immortality of love—and in particular of his love for Arthur Hallam. What, he asks, is the use of all 'the philosophies, all the sciences, poesy, varying voices of prayer':

*What is it all, if we all of us end but in being our own corpse-coffins at last,*
*Swallowed in Vastness, lost in Silence, drown'd in the deeps of a meaningless Past?*

[1] He realized that according to the most recent views of scientists the earth and the whole material universe are only temporary phenomena. Cf. 'Sixty Years After', 'The sun himself will pass'; *In Memoriam*, CXXIII and CXXXI, 'When all that seems shall suffer shock'; and 'Lucretius':

*But till this cosmic order everywhere*
*Shatter'd into one earthquake in one day*
*Cracks all to pieces,—and that hour perhaps*
*Is not so far when momentary man*
*Shall seem no more a something to himself,*
*But he, his hopes and hates, his homes and fanes,*
*And even his bones long laid within the grave,*
*The very sides of the grave itself shall pass,*
*Vanishing, atom and void, atom and void,*
*Into the unseen for ever. . . .*

[2] The statement in the Epilogue to 'The Charge of the Heavy Brigade' (1822) is lighter and less polemical in tone as befits the atmosphere of the poem:

*And tho', in this lean age forlorn,*
*Too many a voice may cry*
*That man can have no after-morn,*
*Not yet of these am I.*
*The man remains, and whatsoe'er*
*He wrought of good or brave*
*Will mould him thro' the cycle-year*
*That dawns behind the grave.*

*What but a murmur of gnats in the gloom, or a moment's anger of bees in their hive?—*

. . . . .

*Peace, let it be! for I loved him and love him for ever: the dead are not dead but alive.*

More than once he repeats with insistence his belief in Love as the guiding force of the universe. In 'Demeter and Persephone' (1889) the Earth Goddess foresees the disappearance of the cruel pagan gods before a new religion of love which is to sweep the world. 'Doubt and Prayer', an early sonnet, but never published before 1889, speaks of:

*. . . That love which was and is*
*My father and my mother and my God.*

and 'Akbar's Dream' tells of the great Emperor's efforts to persuade all the warring sects to sink their differences and worship the God who according to the Christians is Love, and according to the Persians 'The Sun of Love'.

The two most striking and deeply felt of the metaphysical poems of this period and the most closely packed with meaning are undoubtedly 'De Profundis' (*The Two Greetings*) and 'The Ancient Sage'. The former was begun just after the birth of Tennyson's eldest son in 1852, but laid aside and not completed and published until 1880. In the Notes to the annotated Edition of Tennyson's *Works*, pp. 986 *et seq.*, there is an extremely valuable account by Wilfred Ward of a reading of 'De Profundis' by Tennyson himself and the interpretation which he gave to the poem when reading it. This may be summarized as follows: The first part of the poem consists, as its sub-title implies, of two separate greetings to the newly born child, the first viewing life as a purely physical phenomenon, an outcome of all the physical forces of the universe, which have always contained in themselves the potentiality of all that was to come—'all that was to be in all that was'.

. . . These vast and wondrous forces have now issued in this newly given life—this child born into the world. There is the sense of mystery in our greeting to it; but it is of the mysteries of the physical Universe and nothing beyond; the sense of awe fitting to finite man at the thought of infinite Time, of the countless years before human life was at all, during which the fixed laws of Nature were ruling and framing the earth as we know it, of the countless years earlier still, during which, on the nebular hypothesis, Nature's laws were working, before our planet was separated off from the mass of the sun's light and before the similar differentiation took place in the rest of the 'vast waste dawn of multitudinous eddying light'... Forces in Time and Space as nearly infinite as our imagination can conceive, have been leading up to this one birth, with the short life of a single man before it. May that life be happy and noble! Viewing it still as the course determined by Nature's laws—a course unknown to us and yet unalterably fixed—we sigh forth the hope that our child may pass unscathed through youth, may have a full and prosperous time on earth, blessed by man for good done to man, and may pass peacefully at last to rest. . . .

And then comes the second greeting. We leave this wondrous world of appearances. We gaze into that other deep—the world of spirit, the world of realities; we see the new-born babe coming to us from that *true* world, with all 'the abysmal depths of personality', no longer a mere link in the chain of causes, with a fated course through the events of life, but a moral being, with the awful power of making or marring its own destiny and that of others. The proportions are abruptly reversed. The child is no longer the minute outcome of natural forces so much greater than itself. It is the 'spirit', the moral being.

Wilfred Ward records that as Tennyson uttered the word 'spirit' in the seventh line of Part II of the poem, he raised his eyes from the book and fixed them on his hearer with an indescribable expression of awe, and then gave it in deeper and more piercing tones:

*Out of the deep*—Spirit—*out of the deep.*

The second greeting considers the reality of the child's life and its meaning, the first only its appearance. The great deep of the spiritual world is 'that true world within the world we see, whereof our world is but the bounding shore'. The material view looks at bright and hopeful appearances in life, and it notes the new-born babe 'breaking with laughter from the dark'. The spiritual view foresees the woes which, if Byron is right in calling melancholy the 'telescope of truth', are truer than the joys. It notes no longer the child's laughter, but rather its tears. 'Who wailest being born and banished into mystery'. Life, in the spiritual view, is in part a veiling and obscuring of the true self, as it is, in a world of appearances. The soul is 'half lost' in the body which is part of the phenomenal world, 'in thine own shadow and this fleshly sign that thou art thou'. The suns and moons, too, are but shadows, as the body of the child itself is but a shadow—shadows of the spirit-world and of God Himself. The physical life is before the child; but not as a fatally determined course. Choice of the good is to lead the spirit ever nearer God. The wonders of the material Universe are still recognized: 'Sun, sun, and sun, thro' finite-infinite space, in finite-infinite Time'; but they vanish into insignificance when compared to the two great facts of the spirit-world which consciousness tells us unmistakably—the facts of personality and of a responsible will. The great mystery is 'Not Matter, nor the finite-infinite', but '*this main-miracle, that thou art thou, with power on thine own act and on the world*'.

After the second greeting comes a short lyric entitled 'The Human Cry', which Tennyson called a prayer of self-prostration before the Infinite—intended, suggests Wilfred Ward, as a contrast to the analytical and reflective character of the rest of the poem. This, again, is in two parts: the first of five lines, the second of four. In the first the poet hails the Godhead with words as nearly expressive as he can make them of God's infinite qualities:

*Infinite Ideality!*
*Immeasurable Reality!*
*Infinite Personality!*

Not long before his death, when discussing these ideas with his son Hallam, Tennyson said he realized that the insistence on God's personality might be too anthropomorphic, for God must remain unknowable to the finite intelligence of man; but, since personality is the highest development of which man has any knowledge, it must, in some form, be attributed to God.[1] He conceived the

[1] Although he realized to the full the metaphysical difficulties attending the conception of a divine personality, his instinctive realization of God's personality remained unshaken. 'God is walking with us now on this Down, as we two are walking together, just as truly as Christ was with the two disciples on the way to Emmaus,' he said to Agnes Weld when walking with her on the High Down. 'To feel that He is by my side now, as much as you are, that is the very joy of my heart.'

term as including the ideas of 'mind', 'self-consciousness', 'will' and 'Love'.

The last quatrain of the poem is a profound admission of man's insignificance, ending with the words:

*We know we are nothing—but Thou wilt help us to be.*
*Hallowed by Thy name—Hallelujah!*

In 'The Ancient Sage', published in 1885, and written after reading a book of the Life and Maxims of the Chinese philosopher Lao-Tse, Tennyson endeavoured to express what he might have believed about the deeper problems of life, 'A thousand summers ere the time of Christ'. In this way he was able to get down to first principles without having to consider any of the inhibitions and ideas associated with Christian dogma. The poem takes the form of a commentary by a venerable Asiatic philosopher on a poem of singular and corrosive charm, which is handed to him by the young author, a kind of Eastern Alcibiades, who loves and honours the old man and yet is not his disciple. The young man insists on the impossibility of proving the existence of any spiritual power behind the material world, and infers that the only solution for mankind is the familiar pagan precept 'Eat and drink for tomorrow we die'. The old man admits the impossibility of logical proof, but deduces from this the vital necessity for faith.

*Thou canst not prove the Nameless, O my son,*
*Nor canst thou prove the world thou movest in,*
*Thou canst not prove that thou art body alone,*
*Nor canst thou prove that thou art spirit alone,*
*Nor canst thou prove that thou art both in one;*
*Thou canst not prove thou art immortal, no,*
*Nor yet that thou art mortal—nay, my son,*
*Thou canst not prove that I, who speak with thee,*
*Am not thyself in converse with thyself,*
*For nothing worthy proving can be proven,*
*Nor yet disproven: wherefore thou be wise,*
*Cleave ever to the sunnier side of doubt,*[1]
*And cling to Faith beyond the forms of Faith!*

[1] If this seems rather a tepid affirmation, it must be remembered that the speaker was living 'a thousand summers ere the time of Christ'.

*She reels not in the storm of warring words,*
*She brightens at the clash of 'Yes' and 'No',*
*She sees the best that glimmers thro' the worst,*
*She feels the Sun is hid but for a night,*
*She spies the summer thro' the winter bud,*
*She tastes the fruit before the blossom falls,*
*She hears the lark within the songless egg,*
*She finds the fountain where they wailed 'Mirage'!*

He maintains that a solution of life's enigma can only be found by a dive into the Temple-cave of the self—by a resort, for example, to that mystical experience which meant so much to Tennyson himself, and which the old philosopher describes in terms founded on Tennyson's own experience:

. . . *for oft*
*On me, when boy, there came what then I call'd,*
*Who knew no books and no philosophies,*
*In my boy-phrase 'The Passion of the Past'.*
*The first gray streak of earliest summer dawn,*
*The last long stripe of waning crimson gloom,*
*As if the late and early were but one—*
*A height, a broken grange, a grove, a flower,*
*Had murmurs 'Lost and gone and lost and gone!'*
*A breath, a whisper—some divine farewell—*
*Desolate sweetness—far and far away—*
*What had he loved, what had he lost, the boy?*
*I know not and I speak of what has been.*
*And more, my son! for more than once when I*
*Sat all alone, revolving in myself*
*The word that is the symbol of myself,*
*The mortal limit of the Self was loosed,*
*And past into the Nameless, as a cloud*
*Melts into Heaven. I touch'd my limbs, the limbs*
*Were strange not mine—and yet no shade of doubt,*
*But utter clearness, and thro' loss of Self*
*The gain of such large life as match'd with ours*
*Were Sun to spark—unshadowable in words,*
*Themselves but shadows of a shadow world.*

By such intuitions, not greatly different, except for the degree of confidence behind them, from 'the heat of inward evidence' of 'The Two Voices', the old philosopher reaches a serene conclusion:

*My son, the world is dark with griefs and graves,*
*So dark that men cry out against the Heavens.*
*Who knows but that the darkness is in man?*
*The doors of Night may be the gates of Light;*
*For wert thou born or blind or deaf, and then*
*Suddenly heal'd, how would'st thou glory in all*
*The splendours and the voices of the world!*
*And we, the poor earth's dying race, and yet*
*No phantoms, watching from a phantom shore,*
*Await the last and largest sense to make*
*The phantom walls of this illusion fade,*
*And show us that the world is wholly fair.*

Indeed, as Tennyson drew nearer to the end of his life, and particularly after his serious illness of 1888-89, the restless pessimism of 'Locksley Hall, Sixty Years After' seemed to disappear. He reminds himself that although all about him may be 'shadow still' and the time for the consummation of man's development almost infinitely distant:

. . . *While the races flower and fade,*
*Prophet eyes may catch a glory slowly gaining on the shade,*
*Till the peoples all are one, and all their voices blend in choric*
*Hallelujah to the Maker* '*It is finished, Man is made*'.

At the same time a number of short poems show him preparing his spirit for death. Such are the lines *By an Evolutionist* in the volume of 1889:

I

*What hast thou done for me, grim Old Age, save breaking my bones on the rack?*
*Would I had past in the morning that looks so bright from afar!*

*Old Age*

*Done for thee? starved the wild beast that was linkt with thee eighty years back.*
*Less weight now for the ladder of heaven that hangs on a star.*

II

*I have climb'd to the snows of Age, and I gaze at a field in the Past,*
*Where I sank with the body at times in the sloughs of a low desire,*
*But I hear no yelp of the beast, and the Man is quiet at last*
*As he stands on the heights of his life with a glimpse of a height that is higher.*

Such, too, are the short lyrics in his posthumous volume of 1892—'Doubt and Prayer', 'Faith', 'The Silent Voices', and 'God and the Universe'.

Last of all his religious poems one must mention 'Crossing the Bar', which he desired always to be printed at the end of his *Works*, though it was published in 1889. No poem by an English writer ever made so great an impression on the public when it first appeared, as did this lyric of four short stanzas; yet probably few realize the real meaning of the last two lines:

*I hope to see my Pilot face to face*
*When I have crossed the Bar.*

When making them Tennyson had in mind a passenger sailing out of harbour through difficult waters, who does not know that a pilot has been at the wheel, until the ship is out of danger and the pilot comes on deck. 'Crossing the Bar' is therefore not only the moving utterance of a great spirit in the face of death, it is Tennyson's last statement of his unshakable belief in the Divine guidance of the Universe.

In his essay on *In Memoriam* Mr. Eliot says that Tennyson seems to have reached the end of his spiritual development with *In Memoriam*; that there follows 'no reconciliation, no resolution'; that he had nothing to hold on to except his unique and unerring feeling for the sound of words; that he faced neither the darkness nor the light in his later years; that the genius, the technical power continued to the end, but the spirit had surrendered; that he turned aside from the journey through the dark night to become the surface flatterer of his time, with which, though temperamentally opposed to it, he became the most perfect conformist.

I differ from Mr. Eliot with great reluctance, both because of his eminence as a critic and because no contemporary critic has more concisely, convincingly and generously defined Tennyson's greatness. 'Tennyson', he writes at the opening of this essay, 'is a great poet for reasons that are perfectly clear. He has three qualities which are seldom found together except in the greatest poets: abundance, variety and complete competence.' Nevertheless, in the face of the analysis which I have ventured to make of the poems which Tennyson published after *In Memoriam*, I find it very difficult to understand the statements summarized above.

Mr. Eliot's criticism includes a number of rather nebulous phrases of which he offers very little explanation or justification. It seems to be largely based on the suggestion that Tennyson clung to the idea of human perfectibility or progress after he had ceased to believe in it—that indeed he was temperamentally opposed to the doctrine. In this way, it is apparently suggested, he 'flattered' the age which believed in its own progress and in the progressive destiny, based on scientific discovery and material advancement, of the human race.

The statement that Tennyson did not face the darkness, I suppose means that the Poet refused to face what Mr. Eliot possibly conceives to be the truth, that human progress and perfectibility are illusions. The reference to the Poet's refusal to face the light, I imagine implies either that he did not accept the Christian doctrines of original sin and atonement (though whether Mr. Eliot would have him accept them in the Arminian or Calvinistic sense is not clear), or that he could not find a reconciliation in some mystical belief in the unity between God and man which would make all considerations of human destiny irrevelant.

I do not understand how anyone can study Tennyson's references to the subject impartially without coming to the conclusion that his belief in human progress was perfectly sincere and closely linked with the rest of his creed.

The wonder of man's intellectual and moral achievement through the ages, and of the intense struggle against natural instincts and physical limitations, by means of which this had been achieved; the apparent power of the human intellect and imagination, and of the love between man and woman, friend and friend, to transcend the finite and material—such considerations as these made it impossible for him to believe either that the individual soul or spirit would perish with physical death, or that the race would not continue, so long as it existed physically (and he realized that such existence on this planet must some time come to an end), to move, however slowly, upwards towards, though probably never attaining, spiritual perfection.

Perfection would imply rest, and in 'Sixty Years After' Tennyson is careful to speak only of earth reaching her 'earthly best' and to suggest that even if this is attained the 'ideal man' will not be found 'at rest'—i.e., that static perfection can never be reached by humanity. Before earth can reach her 'heavenly best', he says, 'a God must mingle with the game', though he does not rule out the possibility that God may already be active in our own wills without our knowledge.

*Nay there may be those within us whom we neither see nor name,*
*Felt within us as ourselves, the Powers of Good the Powers of Ill,*
*Strowing balm, or shedding poison in the fountains of the Will.*

It may be that he believed in—or did not reject the possibility of —some divine intervention to consummate the process at the last, for in 'The Ancient Sage' he wrote of human civilization as being like all work of man

*A beauty with defect—till That which knows,*
*And is not known, but felt thro' what we feel*
*Within ourselves is highest, shall descend*
*On this half-deed, and shape it at the last*
*According to the Highest in the Highest.*

What form such an intervention might take he did not define either in his poems or, so far as I can discover, in conversation—probably, as suggested in 'Sixty Years After', he contemplated some divinely assisted conquest of the 'Powers of Ill' in the human spirit by the 'Powers of Good'—something that would bring the human will into conformity with the divine. Mr. Eliot says that the hope of immortality is confused in Tennyson's mind (typically of the period) with the hope of gradual and steady improvement of the race. There was no confusion in Tennyson's mind, although, as I have said, the two ideas came from the same source—nor did Tennyson believe (as I shall show later) in a *steady* improvement.

Tennyson certainly 'faced the darkness' by his realization that spiritual progress must from time to time be chequered, as biological progress appeared to be, by 'reversion' to primitive types, and that the age in which he was living was marred by many such reversions. 'Forward still' he wrote in 'Sixty Years After',

> *. . . but still remember how the course of Time will swerve*
> *Crook and turn upon itself in many a backward streaming curve. . . .*

and in *Maud*, the Epilogue to the *Idylls*, 'Sixty Years After', 'Despair' and the 'Promise of May', he castigated what he conceived to be the shortcomings of the age in language which surely never could have been used by a 'surface flatterer' and 'perfect conformist'.

Undoubtedly, as a result both of thought and experience, he came comparatively early to the realization that progress must be agonizingly slow. In 1862 he wrote:

> *Is the goal so far away?*
> *Far, how far no man can say.*
> *Let us dream our dream today.*

Towards the end of his life he repeatedly emphasized that though he still hoped that one day, out of the slow accumulation of knowledge, wisdom and power, there might, as he had foreshadowed in *In Memoriam*, arise

> *. . . . . . . . . the crowning race*
>
> *Of those that, eye to eye, shall look*
> *On knowledge; under whose command*
> *Is Earth and Earth's, and in their hand*
> *Is Nature like an open book;*
>
> *No longer half-akin to brute,*
> *For all we thought and loved and did,*
> *And hoped and suffer'd, is but seed*
> *Of what in them is flower and fruit;*[1]

[1] Tennyson several times made it clear (once, in the Preface to *The Palace of Art*, as early as 1832) that he was not thinking only of material progress and that mere advance in knowledge was insufficient—indeed, unless accompanied by a corresponding spiritual development, actually dangerous.

But he realized that consummation might be almost infinitely distant. This was most clearly stated in the last two stanzas of 'The Dawn' in his posthumous volume:

*Dawn not Day!*
*Is it Shame, so few should have climb'd from the dens in the level below,*
*Men, with a heart and a soul, no slaves of a four-footed will?*
*But if twenty million of summers are stored in the sunlight still,*
*We are far from the noon of man, there is time for the race to grow.*

*Red of the Dawn!*
*Is it turning a fainter red? so be it, but when shall we lay*
*The Ghost of the Brute that is walking and haunting us yet, and be free?*
*In a hundred, a thousand winters? Ah, what will our children be,*
*The men of a hundred thousand, a million summers away?*

On the other hand, as he came nearer to death, he seems to have grown more confident that, by some divine intervention, man would ultimately (if not on this earth, then in the spiritual world) achieve perfection, for in the same posthumous volume he wrote of a time when the moans of the earth, which now whirls through space

*crimson with battles and hollow with graves,*[1]

would have grown 'sphere music', and in 'The Making of Man' he claimed that, though all about us is 'shadow still',

*While the races flower and fade,*
*Prophet eyes may catch a glory slowly gaining on the shade,*
*Till the peoples all are one, and all their voices blend in choric*
*Hallelujah to the Maker 'It is finish'd, Man is made'.*

But this hope for the ultimate perfectibility of man was by no means the main element of Tennyson's faith. To say, as Mr. Eliot does, that he came to 'no reconciliation, no resolution' and had nothing to which to hold fast but his 'unique and unerring feeling for the sounds of words', seems to me, if I may speak so freely of our greatest living man of letters, frankly nonsense. The main pillars of Tennyson's faith were his belief in the guidance of the

[1] In this poem, as in 'Sixty Years After', Tennyson gives antiphonal expression to his own moods of depression and optimism.

Universe by a God who is Love ('for utter knowledge is but utter love' he wrote in 'The Ring'); in the revelation of God's love and the divine law through Jesus Christ[1]; in the immortality of the human spirit, leading to some kind of 'closing' with the divine personality, and in the freedom of the human will. To Mr. Eliot these may seem inadequate concepts, but they did at least lead Tennyson, through the stresses and conflicts of a materialistic and destructive age, to a position of comparative serenity and confidence—and they did, in my view, inspire some of his finest poetry.

[1] 'For love is the fulfilment of the law.' Romans xiii, 10.

## IV

# *Tennyson's Versification*

TENNYSON'S POETIC TECHNIQUE is particularly worth studying because he used such a variety of metres and treated all of them with such remarkable freedom. With few exceptions (mostly at the beginning of his career) he used the accentual type of metre, which has been the normal basis of English poetry since the time of Chaucer. As it will be necessary, in the course of this essay, to refer to other types of metre, I will explain briefly what I consider to be the basis of normal English versification. It may seem strange that this should be thought necessary, but prosody is a difficult and technical subject and there is a good deal of difference between the classifications and definitions used by different schools of thought.

In Latin poetry, which has directly and (through the poetry of Italy and France) indirectly been largely responsible for moulding the form of English versification, metre was based on quantity. Every syllable in the Latin language was held to be either long or short (a few might be used at will as long *or* short), according to a set of generally accepted rules. Following these, the poets evolved regular patterns of sound, and poems were made in these patterns —sometimes, as with the hexameter, every line following the same pattern (subject to variation according to definite rules); sometimes in a pattern covering two successive lines, as in the elegiac metre, e.g. hexameter and pentameter; sometimes in stanza form, e.g. the alcaic and sapphic forms used by Horace. In all these various forms the lines were built up with 'feet', of which the main types were the 'iambic' (short syllable followed by a long syllable), 'anapaest' (two shorts, then one long), 'trochee' (one long followed by one short), 'dactyl' (one long followed by two shorts). There was also a foot called the 'spondee', consisting of two long syllables; but this is very difficult to reproduce in English for reasons which will appear later. The English poets adopted the principles of the Latin poets, substituting for quantity the natural accent of the English language. In the pronunciation of every English word of more than one syllable it will be found that one or more syllables are more heavily accentuated than others, and this accentuation is invariably the same whether the word is pronounced by itself or in a sentence. This can be tested by saying aloud any number of words of more than one syllable. In monosyllables the accentuation (which is more in the nature of the 'stress' mentioned later) varies in accordance with the nature of the word and its position in the sentence. For example, 'the' is very seldom accented. In English versification the accented syllable takes the place of the long syllable in Latin, the unaccented syllables correspond to the short syllables in Latin. As two successive syllables are very seldom, if ever, accented in spoken English, the spondee (foot of two long syllables) practically finds no place in the English scheme; but iambics, anapaests, trochees and dactyls are formed according as one or more unaccented syllables precede or succeed an accented syllable. Manley Hopkins called the feet where the accented comes after the unaccented syllable 'rising rhythms', and those where the accented syllable comes first 'falling rhythms'. But the English poets did not adopt the actual Latin metre patterns (though they have occasionally imitated them—as Tennyson did), they created new patterns more suitable to the genius of the English language. Also they used these patterns with considerable freedom, obtaining beautiful effects by varying the pattern, while being careful never to destroy its essential character. There is another element of great importance to the structure of English verse. In every spoken sentence the voice lays additional stress on certain syllables according to the meaning of the sentence. This stress is quite different from the syllabic *accent* mentioned above, and the relation between it and the syllabic accent is skilfully used by our poets and gives variety and effect to their verses.

Another point in which English verse differs fundamentally from Latin verse is in the use of rhyme, which was unknown in classical Latin poetry, having been first introduced by fourth-century Latin writers of sacred Christian poetry.

To complete the picture it is necessary to say a word about the English poetry which was written before the adoption of the accentual system described above. In this, each line was divided into two parts, each part containing two or more strongly stressed syllables, though more than two are seldom found in the second half. Of these stressed syllables two in the first half and one in the second had to begin with the same letter (to be 'alliterative', to use the technical expression). There was no regular syllabic pattern, considerable freedom being permitted in regard to the number of unstressed syllables included in each half of the line. These unstressed syllables followed no pattern and must have been spoken lightly and rapidly. The following is an example from the Old English poem, *Piers Plowman*:

*In a sómer séson, when sóft was the sónne,*
*I shoóp me into shroúdes, as Í a sheép weere,*
*In hábit as a héremite, unhóly of weérkes. . . .*

Tennyson's first volume, *Poems, Chiefly Lyrical*, published in June 1830, was extraordinarily precocious technically and showed that, however crude in conception some of the poems might be, he had, while little more than a boy (he did not become twenty-one until two months after the book appeared), already fully mastered the principles of English prosody and realized to a surprising degree the possibilities of their application. Of the fifty-six poems which filled the book's 154 pages, only two pairs of antiphonal lyrics ('All things will die' and 'Nothing will die': 'The Merman' and 'The Mermaid') and the few sonnets were identical in metre. Every variety of rhythm was employed, though the 'rising' foot was more common than the 'falling' (as is general in English verse), and both dactyls and anapaests were freely used to give the rhythms speed and lightness. There was one experiment in a strictly classical form (*Leonine Elegiacs*). There was great variety in length of line—lines of 2, 3, 4 and 5 feet being included. There were poems in regular stanzas, and some in the 'Pindaric' form made popular in the seventeenth and eighteenth centuries by Cowley, Dryden, Gray and Collins; though Tennyson's 'Pindarics' are rhythmically very different from those of his predecessors (e.g. 'Ode to Memory' and 'Eleanore'). A large proportion of the poems were in forms which, though constructed on normal principles, had no exact counterpart in the work of earlier poets. Two at least of the lyrics were formal inventions of high excellence, the finest and simplest being 'Mariana', where a striking effect was obtained by making a stanza of eight lines, the first four with alternate rhymes (*a b a b*) and the next four with inclusive rhymes (*a b b a*), followed by a refrain with alternate rhymes.

> *With blackest moss the flower-plots*
> *Were thickly crusted, one and all:*
> *The rusted nails fell from the knots*
> *That held the pear to the gable-wall.*
> *The broken sheds look'd sad and strange:*
> *Unlifted was the clinking latch;*
> *Weeded and worn the ancient thatch*
> *Upon the lonely moated grange.*
> *She only said, 'My life is dreary,*
> *He cometh not,' she said;*
> *She said, 'I am aweary, aweary,*
> *I would that I were dead!'*

Almost equally fine is the 'Song', 'A spirit haunts the year's last hours', where the freer rhythm and the use of alliteration admirably express the sense of the poem:

> *A spirit haunts the year's last hours*
> *Dwelling amid these yellowing bowers:*
> *To himself he talks;*
> *For at eventide, listening earnestly,*
> *At his work you may hear him sob and sigh*
> *In the walks:*
> *Earthward he boweth the heavy stalks*
> *Of the mouldering flowers:*
> *Heavily hangs the broad sunflower*
> *Over its grave i' the earth so chilly;*
> *Heavily hangs the hollyhock,*
> *Heavily hangs the tiger-lily.*

One remarkable feature about the lyrical writing in this volume was the extraordinary freedom of the rhyme schemes. In, for example, 'Isabel', 'Madeline', 'The Arabian Nights', 'Love and Death', 'Margaret' and 'Eleanore', the rhymes seem to flow almost at random and yet to knit the whole poem together very effectively. On the other hand, now and then an unusual regular scheme is used as in 'A Character', where the six-line stanza rhymes *a b c, b c a*.

Of blank verse, which the poet afterwards used on such a large scale, there was only one short example, the six introductory lines to 'The Sea Fairies', but these are very characteristic of the mature Tennyson and show a great advance on the early blank-verse poems such as 'Armageddon' (see above, p. 71):

*Slow sail'd the weary mariners and saw,*
*Betwixt the green brink and the running foam,*
*Sweet faces, rounded arms, and bosoms prest*
*To little harps of gold; and while they mused*
*Whispering to each other half in fear,*
*Shrill music reach'd them on the middle sea.*

But the most interesting metrical feature of this volume was the attempt Tennyson made in a few of the poems to get away from the traditional rhythmic basis of English poetry. He must have been familiar with some Anglo-Saxon poetry—probably *Piers Plowman*, for example—and although he did not anywhere strictly follow the ancient model (particularly in regard to its rigidly regular alliteration), he does seem in some of the poems to have attempted to use the old system of stressed syllables with unstressed syllables grouped round them. Perhaps the most striking examples of this experiment are the two poems 'Nothing will die' and 'All things will die' on pp. 2 and 3 of the *Collected Works*—for example, the following lines from the second poem:[1]

*All things must die.*
*Spring will come never more,*
*Oh! vanity!*
*Death waits at the door.*
*See! our fríends are all forsáking*
*The wíne and the merrymáking.*
*We are cáll'd—we must gó.*
*Laid lów, very lów,*
*In the dárk we must lié.*
*The merry gleés are stíll:*

[1] The accents are inserted by me to show where I suggest that the stress should fall.

*The voíce of the bírd*
*Shall no móre be heárd,*
*Nor the wínd on the híll.*
*Oh! misery!*
*Hark! death is calling*
*While I speak to ye,*
*The jáw is fálling,*
*The réd cheek páling,*
*The stróng limbs faíling:*
*Íce with the warm blood míxing;*
*The eyéballs fíxing.*
*Nine times goes the passing bell:*
*Ye merry souls, farewell.*

Another poem (not reprinted in the *Collected Works*), entitled 'The How and the Why', contains a clear example:

*Why twó and two make fóur? Why róund is not squáre?*
*Why the rócks stand stíll, and the líght clouds flý?*
*Why the heávy oak gróans, and the whíte willows sígh?*
*Why deép is not hígh, and hígh is not deép?*
*Whéther we wáke or whéther we sleép?*
*Whéther we sleép or whéther we díe?*
*Why yoú are yóu? Why Í am Í?*
*Whó will ríddle me the* hów *and the* whý?

These and other instances which occur in the volume of 1830 suggest that Tennyson was trying to find a new basis for English poetry which would combine the old Anglo-Saxon emphasis on leading syllables and the normal emphasis of speech. He discontinued the experiment after 1830, probably because he found that no new system of the kind could provide the musical basis which was, to him, an essential part of poetry. The idea was taken up again thirty or forty years later by Robert Bridges and Gerard Manley Hopkins, and resulted in the evolution of Hopkins's 'sprung rhythm,' which has so greatly influenced modern poetry (for a description of this see *Poems of Gerard Manley Hopkins*, edited by Robert Bridges, Author's Preface, pp. 3 *et seq.*). Meanwhile, Tennyson's experiment called down on him the well-known and absurd stricture of Coleridge, that he had begun writing poetry without any clear idea what metre was. Tennyson's comment on this showed that he did not attach much importance to his early experiments. He admitted that he had in his youth 'played some tricks with metre', but said that Coleridge should have known it was 'due to wantonness not ignorance'.

Tennyson's second volume (published at the end of 1832, but dated 1833) was much more substantial than his first, containing about half the number of poems in a greater number of pages, and shows the poet settling down into the lines of progress which he was to follow for the remainder of his life. There were several important lyrical poems which, though not all of them had yet reached the perfection to which subsequent revision brought them, showed that his grasp of structure and rhythm was increasing. 'The Lady of Shalott' was a metrical *tour de force*, written in a stanza of seven lines, the first four all with the same rhyme ending and the last three also with one, though a different, rhyme ending, and a refrain after the third and fourth lines. This difficult metre, which was handled with great lightness and freedom, gave the poem an extraordinary speed and 'punch'. 'The Two Voices',[1] on the other hand, which describes a dialogue between a would-be suicide and the still small voice of the tempter, is composed in a stanza of three short lines with a single rhyme, and written with a sledgehammer regularity which gives the dialogue an extraordinary and rather terrifying insistence. 'The Palace of Art' and 'The Dream of Fair Women' each present a series of pictures, the second considerably more dramatic than the first. They are composed in slightly different four-line stanzas, the slow, rich movement of which gives the effect of tapestry. Most striking of all was 'The Lotus Eaters'. Here the introductory lines are in the Spenserian stanza (the only use of this classical English rhythm in Tennyson's published works), but handled so freely that very few readers recognize it. The most famous part of the poem, the 'Choric Song', is written in iambic lines which vary in length—between three feet and seven feet. The rhythm is plentifully varied by the inversion of iambics into trochees, and in the sixth line of the last Section (VIII) it suddenly becomes entirely trochaic,

[1] 'The Two Voices' was not written until a year or more after the publication of the volume of 1833, and not published until 1842. I deal with it here as it can be usefully and conveniently compared with the long lyrics of 1833.

with striking effect: 'we have had enough of action and of motion we', etc. The poem thus foreshadows the metrical method of *Maud* (although anapaests are hardly used at all), the rhythm adapting itself with extraordinary spontaneity to the fluctuating emotions of the theme, and yet preserving continuity and harmony of style. In addition to these great lyrics, which Tennyson never surpassed, the volume contained the earliest examples of his popular ballads—'The Miller's Daughter' and 'The May Queen'. The second of these poems foreshadowed the technique which he was to apply to all the popular ballads of his later life—'The First Quarrel', 'Rizpah', 'In the Children's Hospital', 'Despair', and so on. It is written in a rising rhythm of seven iambics, irregularly varied by anapaests, by the inversion of a foot (particularly at the beginning of the line), by the use of a single suspended syllable in the middle of the line, and by the variation of the caesura or natural sense-break in the line. A remarkable instance of inversion is the first line of the poem; this is really trochaic throughout:

> *You must wake and call me early, call me early, Mother dear.*

The variation of caesura is very frequent:

> *He thought I was a ghost, mother, | for I was all in white,*
> *And I ran by him without speaking | like a flash of light.*

In the second line the caesura comes one syllable later than in the first.

Another important feature of his second volume was the inclusion of the first of the mature poems in blank verse, 'Oenone'. This I will discuss later when I deal with Tennyson's blank verse, which can best be considered as a separate subject.

A point of minor interest is that the metre of *In Memoriam* appeared in this volume for the first time in a brief lyric called 'The Blackbird'. This metre was not Tennyson's invention, having been used by Ben Jonson, Lord Herbert of Cherbury and others, though Tennyson seems not to have been aware of this earlier use. The rhythm in 'The Blackbird' seems very different from that of *In Memoriam*, being much more lightly handled, though the chief characteristic, the enclosed rhyme, *ab ba*, is the same in both poems. Another poem in the 1833 volume ('to J.S.') seems much more like *In Memoriam*, because of the similarity of subject and atmosphere, although the rhyme scheme is different —the normal *a b a b* arrangement. A very interesting poem is 'The Vision of Sin'. The first two sections of this contain the only extended use of the heroic couplet in Tennyson's mature work.[1] The rhythm is, however, so lightly handled with so many inversions and clauses overrunning the end of the couplet, that few readers recognize it. In the course of the second section the rhythm grows freer and wilder, until it changes into a four-foot trochaic line irregularly rhymed. After other variations designed to express the changing emotions of the poem, the final section (v) reverts to the heroic couplet in a more serene and regular form.

One poem in this volume which is metrically most interesting, was not reprinted by Tennyson, and appeared for the first time in Hallam Tennyson's *Memoir* (single volume edition, p. 52)—the long lyric entitled 'The Hesperides'. Its rhythm does not, like that of Tennyson's earlier experiments, depend on the old Anglo-Saxon principle (though there is an analogous use of the stressed or emphatic syllables in some of the lines which I have marked with accents in the quotations which follow) but observes the traditional accentual method so far as the individual lines are concerned. But there is no regular pattern either of stanza or individual lines, these varying in length and rhythm on what I can only describe as a musical basis; that is to say, like the melodic line of a very free musical composition. The second section of this remarkable rhythmic invention well illustrates its quality:

*Father Hesper, Father Hesper, watch, watch, ever and aye,*
*Looking under silver hair with a silver eye.*
*Father, twinkle not thy stedfast sight;*
*Kingdoms lápse, and climates chánge, and races díe;*
*Honour comes with mystery;*
*Hoarded wisdom brings delight.*
*Númber, téll them óver and númber*
*How many the mystic fruit-tree holds,*
*Lest the redcombed dragon slumber*
*Rolled together in purple folds.*

[1] In *Unpublished Early Poems*, p. 1, there is a brilliantly effective, if conventional, translation from the Proserpine of Claudian into this metre, made when Tennyson was thirteen or fourteen.

*Look to him, father, lest he wink, and the golden apple be stol'n*
*away,*
*For his ancient heart is drunk with overwatchings night and day,*
*Round about the hallowed fruit tree curled—*
*Sing awáy, sing aloúd evermóre in the wínd, without stóp,*
*Lest his scalèd eyelid drop,*
*For he is older than the world.*
*If hé waken, wé waken,*
*Rapidly levelling eager eyes.*
*If hé sleep, wé sleep,*
*Dropping the eyelid over the eyes.*
*If the golden apple be taken*
*The world will be overwise.*
*Five links, a golden chain, are we,*
*Hesper, the dragon, and sisters three,*
*Bound about the golden tree.*

At about the same time Tennyson made another experiment on similar lines, the poem 'Ilion, Ilion'. This he never published, and it appeared for the first time in *Early Unpublished Poems* (1931). This is even freer in form than 'The Hesperides', but seems to follow the same principles. I have accented the emphatic syllables to show how I think the lines should be read.

*Ilion, Ilion*

*Ílion, Ílion, dréamy Ilion, píllared Ilion, hóly Ilion,*
*Cíty of Ílion whén wilt thoú be mélody bórn?*
*Blué Scamánder, yéllowing Símois from the heárt of píny Ída*
*Everwhírling from the mólten snóws upon the moúntainthróne,*
*Róll Scamánder, rípple Símois, ever ónward to a mélody*
*Manycírcled, overflówing thóro' and thóro' the flówery lével of únbuilt Ílion,*
*Cíty of Ílion, píllared Ílion, shádowy Ilion, hóly Ilion,*
*To a músic merrily flówing, merrily échoing*
*Whén wilt thoú be mélody bórn?*
*Manygáted, heavywálled, manytówered cíty of Ílion,*
*From the sílver, lilyflówering meadowlével*
*Whén wilt thoú be mélody born?*
*Ripple ónward echoing Símois,*

*Ripple éver with a mélancholy móaning*
*In the rúshes to the dárk blue brímméd Ócean, yéllowing Símois,*
*To a músic from the gólden twánging hárpwire héavily dráwn.*
*Manygáted, heavywálled, manytówered, cíty of Ílion,*
*To a músic sádly flówing, slówly fálling,*
*Whén wilt thoú be mélody bórn?*

Tennyson never pushed this line of development any further. Probably he felt that the gain in freedom did not compensate for what was lost through diffuseness and the lack of a comprehensive and distinctive form for the poem as a whole; but there is no doubt (as I shall suggest later) that he learned a great deal from the experiment.

Within nine months of the publication of the volume of 1833 Arthur Hallam died, and Tennyson, shattered by his loss, and depressed by the critical attacks on his poetry, published no more until 1842, when he brought out two volumes, the first containing a revised selection of his earlier work and the second entirely new poems. The latter showed a remarkable change from the poet's previous work. Nearly one-third of its 231 pages were occupied by blank-verse poems, with which I will deal later. There were many admirable lyrics which, however, displayed no metrical innovations. (I have already dealt with 'The Two Voices', which first appeared in this volume.) After the blank-verse poems the most striking novelty was the long poem in trochaic (falling) rhythm, 'Locksley Hall', with a line of eight feet (sixteen syllables normally). This was the first trochaic poem of importance that Tennyson had published (there were some short lyrics with a trochaic basis in his first volume, e.g. 'Lilian', 'The Poet's Mind' and 'The Deserted House'), and it has been criticized for the excessive rigidity of its rhythm. One may be certain that this rigidity was intentional. The poem is an impassioned and rather hysterical protest against the social and spiritual conditions of the day spoken by a young man, who has been jilted by his betrothed. It has to be read at a rattling pace and with the maximum of dramatic expression. The regularity of the beat helps to give the sense of speed and enables the rhythm to be maintained, however intense the drama of the reading. The volume contained one other trochaic poem written in lines of four feet, 'The Lord of Bur-

K

leigh'. Tennyson used the trochaic basis sparingly. Apart from the Continuation of 'Locksley Hall' ('Sixty Years After'), published in 1886, he only employed it in a few short poems, e.g. the song 'Hapless doom of woman' in *Queen Mary*, Act v, Sc. 2; 'The Captain' (1865); 'The City Child', published 1880 (but written for *The Princess* before 1850); 'Frater Ave atque Vale' (1883); 'Forlorn' and 'The Snowdrop' (1889); 'The Tourney', 'Faith', 'Poets and Critics', 'The Making of Man', 'God and the Universe' (1892). 'Forlorn' and 'Poets and Critics' are early poems in spite of their late publication. There are two dactylic songs in the plays, viz. the duet at the opening of *Becket*, Act II, Sc. 1, and Camma's song in Act I, Sc. 2, of *The Cup*. 'Vastness' (1889) and 'The Dawn' (1892) are late dactylic poems.

It must, however, be admitted that it is not always easy to be sure how an English poet intends an apparently trochaic rhythm to be read, since the placing of an accented syllable at the beginning of an iambic line makes it apparently trochaic, but if this syllable is read lightly and, so to speak, held in suspense, the iambic character is retained. It was for this reason that Manley Hopkins suggested that the accented syllable should always be taken as the beginning of the rhythm (any preceding syllable or syllables being suspended) and the possible feet in English verse thereby reduced to two, the trochee and the dactyl. This is undoubtedly a simplification, but I think a misleading one, as it seems to me that the poets generally intend a rising (iambic or anapaestic) rhythm (e.g. in blank verse and the rhyming heroic couplet and most of the normal stanza forms).

Tennyson's next publication after the volumes of 1842 was the long blank verse poem *The Princess* (1847), which I will consider in my study of his blank verse. After that came *In Memoriam* in 1850, the *annus mirabilis* which also saw his marriage and appointment as Poet Laureate.

Metrically (as well as in many other respects) one would think that the stanza of *In Memoriam* (which I have already described) of four Iambic lines of four feet each, with enclosed rhymes (*a b b a*) would be unendurably monotonous in a poem of about 3000 lines, and if Tennyson, when he began writing the poem, had foreseen what its total length was going to be, he would probably have chosen a different form. But *In Memoriam* developed and grew more or less haphazard over a period of seventeen years. Beginning immediately after Arthur Hallam's death at the end of 1833, Tennyson jotted down stanzas and short poems from time to time as they occurred to him and never thought of publishing these 'elegies', as he called them, until he found, towards the end of the 'forties, how much he had written and how easily the various poems might be fitted into a harmonious whole. Treated in this way, the *In Memoriam* stanza is surprisingly successful. The subject is one which needs a slow and majestic rhythm and even a certain monotony, and Tennyson succeeded in giving it such variation as was necessary and adapting it to the changing moods of his poem, by a skilful use of vowel music and alliteration: by occasional inversions of rhythm: by running the sense over from line to line and even from stanza to stanza, and other such devices. To realize what the metre is capable of in his hands, one has only to contrast 'The Blackbird' with Section LXXXVI of *In Memoriam* (which he was fond of making his friends read as a test of their power to speak verse).

### *The Blackbird*

*O blackbird! sing me something well:*
*While all the neighbours shoot thee round,*
*I keep smooth plats of fruitful ground,*
*Where thou may'st warble, eat and dwell.*

*The espaliers and the standards all*
*Are thine; the range of lawn and park;*
*The unnetted black-hearts ripen dark,*
*All thine, against the garden wall.*

*Yet, tho' I spared thee all the spring,*
*Thy sole delight is, sitting still,*
*With that gold dagger of thy bill*
*To fret the summer jenneting.*

*A golden bill! the silver tongue,*
*Cold February loved, is dry:*
*Plenty corrupts the melody*
*That made thee famous once, when young:*

*And in the sultry garden squares,*
*Now thy flute-notes are changed to coarse,*
*I hear thee not at all, or hoarse*
*As when a hawker hawks his wares.*

*Take warning! he that will not sing*
*While yon sun prospers in the blue,*
*Shall sing for want, ere leaves are new,*
*Caught in the frozen palms of Spring.*

*In Memoriam,*
LXXXVI

*Sweet after showers, ambrosial air,*
*That rollest from the gorgeous gloom*
*Of evening over brake and bloom*
*And meadow, slowly breathing bare*

*The round of space, and rapt below*
*Thro' all the dewy-tassell'd wood,*
*And shadowing down the horned flood*
*In ripples, fan my brows and blow*

*The fever from my cheek, and sigh*
*The full new life that feeds thy breath*
*Throughout my frame, till Doubt and Death,*
*Ill brethren, let the fancy fly*

*From belt to belt of crimson seas*
*On leagues of odour streaming far,*
*To where in yonder orient star*
*A hundred spirits whisper 'Peace'.*

The years from the publication of *The Princess* (1847) to 1855 saw the culmination of Tennyson's lyric genius, including, in addition to the introductory stanzas and closing sections of *In Memoriam*, the famous songs placed between the Cantos of *The Princess* (1850), the 'Ode on the Death of the Duke of Wellington' and *Maud*.

In the Wellington Ode Tennyson put into practice what he had learned through his early experiments in 'The Hesperides' and 'Ilion, Ilion'. The Ode is just as truly melodic[1] as either of the earlier poems, but it has a more coherent form, so that interest and emotion are concentrated instead of being dispersed and distracted. But the form is exceedingly free. The poem is composed of nine sections of very unequal length, the longest comprising 77 lines, the shortest only 5. The metre is iambic, occasionally varied with anapaests and sometimes given a trochaic quality by the inversion of the first foot (note that in Section V the words 'Lét the béll be tóll'd' must be read with three beats to suggest the sound of the bell), and the lines vary in length from three to five feet. The use of vowel sound and rhyme is exceedingly skilful and varied. The two five-line sections (II and III) have each a single rhyme throughout; elsewhere rhymes occur in pairs or in groups of three, four or five, or are distributed in irregular patterns. The melodic line is freely and beautifully varied to express the emotions of the poem, and the musical form is emphasized by what one may call the Handelian close of Sections V, VI and VIII. Some idea of the poem's quality and method may be gained from the lines in the sixth section addressed to Nelson, which describe the Battle of Waterloo:

*Again their ravening eagle rose*
*In anger, wheel'd on Europe-shadowing wings,*
*And barking for the thrones of kings;*
*Till one that sought but Duty's iron crown*
*On that loud sabbath shook the spoiler down;*
*A day of onsets of despair!*
*Dash'd on every rocky square*
*Their surging charges foam'd themselves away;*
*Last, the Prussian trumpet blew;*
*Thro' the long-tormented air*
*Heaven flashed a sudden jubilant ray,*

[1] Tennyson used to emphasize the melodic nature of the Ode by the way in which he chanted it when reading it aloud. In certain passages he would suddenly raise the pitch of his voice several notes with surprising effect, e.g. Section II, 'Where shall we lay the man whom we deplore' to end of the section, and the last five lines of Section IV, 'O fall'n at length', etc.

*And down we swept and charged and overthrew.*
*So great a soldier taught us there,*
*What long-enduring hearts could do*
*In that world-earthquake, Waterloo!*
*Mighty Seaman, tender and true,*
*And pure as he from taint of craven guile,*
*O saviour of the silver-coasted isle,*
*O shaker of the Baltic and the Nile,*
*If aught of things that here befall*
*Touch a spirit among things divine,*
*If love of country move thee there at all,*
*Be glad, because his bones are laid by thine!*
*And thro' the centuries let a people's voice*
*In full acclaim,*
*A people's voice,*
*The proof and echo of all human fame,*
*A people's voice, when they rejoice*
*At civic revel and pomp and game,*
*Attest their great commander's claim*
*With honour, honour, honour, honour to him,*
*Eternal honour to his name.*

In the next poem which he published, *Maud*, Tennyson applied to an intensely dramatic subject the method which had made his threnody for the Great Duke so memorable. *Maud* is a lyrical monologue reflecting in about 1200 passionate lines a story of love, death and madness. The metre has, like that of the Ode, an iambic base, plentifully varied with anapaests; only one or two short sections are in a trochaic (falling) rhythm, e.g. 'go not, happy day', Part I, XVII, and the Shell lyric, Part II, II. The lines vary in length from six feet to three and the rhyme schemes are exceedingly fluid and so well managed that, although the rhyme is hardly ever obtrusive, it never fails to act as an effective link in the chain of sound. By these means Tennyson evolved a form of extraordinary speed, fluency and adaptability. The range of its expressiveness can be seen by comparing the grim repressed rhythms of the opening (Part I, first four stanzas), the lover's ecstasy of Part I, Sect. XVIII (1), the swinging dance rhythm of 'Come into the garden, Maud', Part I, XXII, and the martial sweep of Part III, which leaves the hero volunteering for service in the Crimean War.

*Maud* marked the end of Tennyson's great lyrical period. After it he wrote many beautiful lyrics, including the most famous of all his short poems, 'Crossing the Bar', but he was now nearing fifty years old and his creative energy turned in new directions.

A word must, however, be said about his imitations of classical and other metres.

The 'Leonine Elegiacs' in the volume of 1830 have little merit from a metrical point of view. His first important 'experiments in quantity', as he rightly called them, appeared in the 'Enoch Arden' volume of 1864. These included some elegiacs 'On Translations of Homer', the 'Alcaics to Milton', the 'Hendecasyllabics' 'Oh, you chorus of indolent reviewers', and the long poem 'Boadicea'. A late example occurs in the 'Ode on the Jubilee of Queen Victoria' (*Works*, p. 843), Sections II, IV, VI, VIII and X. Here Tennyson imitated quantitatively the metre of Catullus's marriage song of Manlius Torquatus.

Although, as I have already suggested, English poetry is based on the accent which we place on certain syllables of the words which we speak, the syllables which make up our English words have, in theory at least, long and short quantity, in the same way that Latin words had, although in our language no rules have ever been laid down by which English quantities can be defined. Tennyson himself once said that he knew the quantities in every English word except perhaps 'scissors'; other scholars have been less sanguine and some discussion on the subject will be found in the Foreword to Robert Bridges's *Poems in Classical Prosody* (*Poetical Works of Robert Bridges*, 1914, p. 410). The difficulty of using a quantitative basis in writing English verse is that this often conflicts with the accent and it is very hard to adjust the conflict satisfactorily. Bridges obtained some curious and subtle effects in his experiments, though it is often very difficult to detect any resemblance to the Classical original. The following versions of three well-known lines from Virgil's *Æneid*, Bk. VI, are good examples:

*They wer' amid the shadows by night in loneliness obscure.*
*Walking forth i' the void and vasty dominyon of Ades.*
*As by an uncertain moonray secretly illumin'd.*

In these lines accent and quantity are allowed to conflict freely. This method did not appeal to Tennyson, and in his experiments (I exclude 'Boadicea' from this statement) he took the trouble to make accent and quantity coincide. The result is that his lines move with remarkable ease and spontaneity and, in fact, to the casual reader, do not seem to differ at all in *method* from normal English verse, though of course the metres are different. This applies particularly to the 'Alcaics to Milton' (and Tennyson in a note particularly asked that his readers would *not* pronounce the great poet's name as 'Milt'n'!). The hendecasyllables (following a favourite metre of Tennyson's favourite Catullus) are less rigidly quantitative.

With the Milton 'Alcaics' may be contrasted two other poems based on this Latin metre, but freer in adaptation: 'The Daisy' and 'To the Rev. F. D. Maurice' (*Works*, pp. 233 and 234). These are not quantitative experiments, but follow the normal accentual method of English verse.

'Boadicea' is an adaptation—'a far-off echo', Tennyson called it—of the very remarkable metre used in Catullus's poem 'Attis'. The correct scansion of Tennyson's lines is a matter of some controversy, because they appear, whether read according to quantity or accent, to conflict in one or two important respects with Catullus's metre, the essence of which is that the line begins with two short hurrying syllables and ends with five short syllables—an effect almost impossible to secure in English, since we never pronounce five successive syllables without strongly accentuating at least one of them. Tennyson does his best to finish off his lines with five quantitatively short syllables, and to lighten their accentuation by forming the sentence so that a heavy stress falls naturally on the syllable which immediately precedes them. But he more often than not begins the line with a syllable that is long in quantity and occasionally with one which is naturally accented in speech. He himself gave no clue how he wished his poem to be read, except by saying optimistically that, if it was read 'straight like prose, it would come all right'! My own view is that where possible one should throw a strong accent on the third syllable of the line and on the sixth syllable from the end. This is not always possible or suitable, but the important thing is not to read the poem as though it were a rather clumsy variant of the 'Locksley

Hall' metre. When once the rhythm is mastered it is a fine poem to read aloud and does, in spite of its occasional variants, give a good representation of Catullus's remarkable *tour de force*.

Tennyson wrote one or two poems in imitation of other alien metres, e.g. 'The Battle of Brunanburh' (*Works*, p. 534) and the remarkable autobiographical lyric, 'Merlin and the Gleam' (*Works*, p. 867). Neither of these attempts a technical imitation of the Anglo-Saxon stress rhythm, but only 'a far-off echo'.

Another very interesting experiment is 'Kapiolani', which appeared in Tennyson's posthumous volume of 1892. This describes the heroic action of a Hawaiian Queen who converted her people to Christianity by breaking the taboo and challenging the authority of the priesthood. It is founded on a story in Miss Young's *Golden Deeds*, but I believe that in rhythm it is an attempt to recapture the swing of the Hawaiian songs, which Tennyson had heard from the retinue of Queen Emma of the Sandwich Islands, when she visited him at Farringford in 1865, and her vast henchman, Mr. Hoapili, used to squat on the drawing-room floor and sing native ballads to the twanging of a Samoan lute.

After 1855, Tennyson's poetic activity took three main forms: the *Idylls of the King*, which I will consider with the rest of his blank verse, the dramas, which lie outside the scope of this essay, and the Ballads, which I have already mentioned in connexion with 'The May Queen'. These are of three types: the two great battle stories—'The Revenge' and 'The Defence of Lucknow', the poems in the Lincolnshire dialect, and the miscellaneous ballads, including 'Rizpah', 'The Grandmother', 'The Children's Hospital', and so on. All of these poems are in iambic metres, broken up, by means which I have already sufficiently described, to adjust them to the character of the speaker and the nature of the subject. Only two are entirely composed in 'The May Queen' line of seven feet—'The Flight' (*Works*, p. 552) and 'Happy' or 'The Leper's Bride' (*Works*, p. 860). In 'The Revenge', which is much the most interesting metrically of the whole group, lines of seven, six and five feet are used. The remainder, 'The Grandmother', the two 'Northern Farmers', 'The First Quarrel', 'Rizpah', 'The Northern Cobbler', 'The Village Wife', 'The Spinster's Sweet-Arts', 'In the Children's Hospital', 'The Defence of Lucknow', 'The Wreck', 'Despair', 'Tomorrow', 'Owd Roa', 'The

Bandit's Death', 'The Churchwarden and the Curate' and 'Charity', all have a line of six feet and are basically identical in metre with *Maud*, Part I, Sections I, II, III and IV, though this identity is hard to realize owing to the skill with which Tennyson varied the rhythm to suit the spirit and atmosphere of the different poems. It is remarkable that a poet, who was always so careful to adjust the form of a poem to its subject should have used the same metre for so large a number of widely differing poems. They have, however, all of them one element in common: they need intensely dramatic reading, whether tragic, comic or sentimental. It seems that Tennyson felt that poems of this kind required a strong and insistent rhythm to hold them together—and, in the case of the comic poems, to emphasize their points—and he had such complete control of this metre that he could use it with perfect spontaneity and freedom. Moreover, he was able by the poetic devices of which he was so great a master to give the six-foot line an endless variety of rhythm and colour, so that when one reads the poems through it is often difficult to realize their metrical similarity. Whether one admires this type of poem or not (and some of them at least, e.g. the two 'Farmers', 'The Village Wife', 'The Northern Cobbler', 'Rizpah', 'The Revenge', and 'The Defence of Lucknow', are, I think, among Tennyson's best work), one cannot help recognizing the skill of the versification.

It remains now to consider Tennyson's blank verse. This is, in volume, far the most substantial part of his work. Excluding the plays, more than half of his total output is in blank verse. If the plays are included, the proportion is nearly two-thirds.

Before proceeding to study the blank verse in detail, it is well to realize the principles on which he composed it. The normal blank-verse line is composed of five iambic feet, which make ten syllables in all, e.g.

*The life | that had | descen|ded re|arise|.*

But a normal line does not often occur, for too frequent use of the normal rhythm produces monotony. Poets, therefore, diversify their lines by the free use of inversions, by substituting two short (or unaccented) syllables for one long (or accented) syllable, and various other means. As a result blank verse lines sometimes have eleven, twelve, or even thirteen syllables, e.g.

*Scatter'd | all o|ver the | vocab|ulary.|*
(Eleven syllables)
*Fingering | at his | sword han|dle until | he stood.|*
(Twelve syllables)
*Pricked with | incre|dible pin|nacles in|to heaven.|*
(Thirteen syllables)

Tennyson used all these devices very freely. But there is another element of great importance in his blank verse. Some light is thrown on this by a rather cryptic note in the annotated edition of the *Works*, pp. 962 and 963. This runs as follows:

'Examples of blank verse

with three beats
*And Bálin by the bánneret of his hélm*
with four beats
*For háte and loáthing would have pássed him bý.*
with five beats
*In whích he scárce could spý the Chríst for saínts*
with six beats
*Whát, weár ye stíll that sáme crówn scándalous?*
with seven beats
*The twó-célled héart beáting with oné fúll stróke.*'

The 'beats' referred to here are obviously what I have at the beginning of this essay called 'the sentence stress', i.e. the stress which the speaker naturally lays on certain words in the sentence in order to emphasize its meaning. I infer from this that one of Tennyson's principal aims in his blank verse was to create a tension between the accentual stress of the rhythm and the sentence stress. If this is borne in mind in reading Tennyson's blank verse (and the method is, of course, by no means confined to Tennyson), it will be found that the verse acquires a pattern which often spreads over long verse paragraphs, and gives the writing a continuity and force which will be missed if the reader allows himself to emphasize the accentual rhythm too exclusively and to make a pause at the end of each line.

All great poets have their special fields of excellence, and it is difficult to compare one usefully with another. Tennyson's blank verse has not the majesty of Milton's, nor the rhetorical splendour and freedom of Shelley's (and I use the word 'rhetorical' in no derogatory sense), nor the natural eloquence and dignity of Wordsworth's; but it has striking merits of its own, chief among which are, I think, its amazing flexibility and its power of achieving, through rhythm and vowel music, a lyrical, singing quality which no other poet has attained in the same degree. The lyrical quality appeared strikingly in 'Oenone', one of his earliest long poems in this metre, the first few lines of which (in the revised form in which they appeared in 1842) provide an admirable example, if they are read (as they must be) with due emphasis on the broad and open vowel sounds.

*There is a vale in Ida, lovelier*
*Than all the vallies of Ionian hills.*
*The swimming vapour slopes athwart the glen,*
*Puts forth an arm and creeps from pine to pine,*
*And loiters slowly drawn. . . .*

One could quote innumerable examples, such as the opening of 'Morte d'Arthur':

*So all day long the noise of battle rolled*

and of Tithonus:

*The woods decay, the woods decay and fall,*
*The vapours weep their burdens to the ground,*
*Man comes and tills the field and lies beneath,*
*And after many a summer dies the swan.*

Perhaps the most striking examples of all are the blank-verse lyrics in *The Princess*—a type of composition which, I think, Tennyson can be said to have created. These short poems are so lyrical in quality that probably few readers realize that they are written in blank verse. I refer to '*Tears, Idle Tears*', and '*O Swallow, Swallow*' in Canto IV, '*Our enemies have fallen*' in Canto VI and '*Now sleeps the crimson petal*' and '*Come down, O maid . . .*' in Canto VII. Tennyson also included blank-verse lyrics in 'Audley Court'—two examples (*Works*, p. 79), and 'The Golden Year'

(*Works*, p. 94). To get the full value out of such verse, one must not be afraid of emphasizing the rhythm and the vowel sounds.

But this quality, beautiful as it is in lyrical passages, is necessarily limited in its application, and it is the flexibility of Tennyson's verse and his varied control of rhythm that enabled him to use the metre successfully for so many different types of poem—for example, the almost conversational *English Idyls*, the nostalgic richness of 'The Gardener's Daughter', the austere and restrained emotion of 'Dora', the comedy, drama and burlesque of *The Princess*; for poems of occasion, such as the lines to the Prince Consort (*Works*, p. 308) and the Dedication to the poet's wife 'Dear, near and true' (*Works*, p. 240) and for the infinitely diversified narrative of the *Idylls of the King*.

Critics have sometimes found a too deliberate artistry and refinement in Tennyson's blank verse, particularly that of the *English Idyls* and the later *Idylls of the King*, a kind of criticism which is delightfully illustrated in Calverley's parody of 'The Brook'; for example, the poet's farewell to the tramp, who takes the place of the 'babbling brook' in Tennyson's poem:

> *Then I 'The sun has sunk behind the hill*
> *And my Aunt Vivian dines at half past six.'*
> *So all in love we parted, I to the Hall*
> *He to the village. It was noised next day*
> *That chickens had been missed at Syllabub Farm.*

Tennyson himself had perhaps something of this sort in mind when, in a moment of despondency, he referred to 'the foolish facility of Tennysonian verse'; but this facility, combined with his unrivalled control of the medium, gave his verse a flexibility and range which is unrivalled by any other poet. One has only to contrast a few typical examples to realize the truth of this: for instance, the romantic opening lines of 'Morte d'Arthur':

> *So all day long the noise of battle rolled*
> *Among the mountains by the winter sea*

with the conversational introductory poem 'The Epic', which immediately precedes it:

*At Francis Allen's on the Christmas Eve,*
*The game of forfeits done—the girls all kiss'd*
*Beneath the sacred bush and past away. . . .*

the stark simplicity of 'Dora' with the hectic and contorted ravings of 'St. Simeon'; the noble declamation of the lines to the Prince Consort with the singing lyricism of 'Come down, O maid' from Canto VII of *The Princess*; the speed and lucidity of the translation from the *Iliad*:

*So Hector spake: the Trojans roared applause;*
*Then loosed their sweating horses from the yoke,*
*And each beside his chariot bound his own . . .*

with the frenzied crash of the mad Lucretius' vision:

*Storm in the night! for thrice I heard the rain*
*Rushing; and once the flash of a thunderbolt—*
*Methought I never saw so fierce a fork—*
*Struck out the streaming mountainside, and shewed*
*A riotous confluence of watercourses*
*Blanching and billowing in the hollow of it . . .*
*. . . . for it seemed*
*A void was made in nature; all her bonds*
*Cracked; and I saw the flaring atom streams*
*And torrents of her myriad universe,*
*Ruining along the illimitable inane,*
*Fly on and clash together again and make*
*Another and another frame of things*
*For ever. . . .*

In addition to these broad and striking contrasts of rhythm, Tennyson's delicate ear enabled him to enhance his verse with innumerable felicities of detail, creating, by subtle variations of rhythm and vowel sound, mental and sensual images to reinforce the literal meaning of his words. *The Princess* and the *Idylls of the King* provide countless examples of such felicity.

E.g. *The Princess*:

*. . . round the lake*
*A little clockwork steamer paddling plied*
*And shook the lilies. . . .* (Prologue.)

(of a set of oriental puzzle-boxes, one inside the other)

*Laborious orient ivory sphere in sphere*

(Prologue.)

*The broad ambrosial aisles of lofty elm*
*Made noise of bees and breeze from end to end*

(Prologue.)

*. . . as when a boat tacks*
*And the sail flaps, all her voice*
*Faltering and fluttering in her throat, she cried. . . .*

(Canto II.)

*Strove to buffet to land in vain. . . .*

(Canto IV.)

*The horses yell'd; they clashed their arms; the drum*
*Beat; merrily-blowing shrilled the martial fife;*
*And in the blast and bray of the long horn*
*And serpented-throated bugle, undulated*
*The banner. . . .*

(Canto V.)

*When storm is on the heights, and right and left*
*Suck'd from the dark heart of the long hills roll*
*The torrents, dash'd to the vale. . . .*

(Canto V.)

*Pledge of a love, not to be mine, farewell*

(Canto VII.)

From the *Idylls of the King*:

*The hoof of his horse slipt in the stream, the stream*
*Descended and the Sun was washed away.*

(Gareth and Lynette.)

*. . . Everywhere*
*Was hammer laid to hoof, and the hot hiss*
*And bustling whistle of the youth who scoured*
*His master's armour; . . .*

(Geraint and Enid.)

*. . . then did either side,*
*They that assail'd, and they that held the lists,*
*Set lance in rest, strike spur, suddenly move,*
*Meet in the midst, and there so furiously*
*Shock. . . .*

(Lancelot and Elaine.)

*First as in fear, step after step, she stole*
*Down the long tower-stairs, hesitating. . . .*

(*Ib.*)

*. . . when out of heaven a bolt*
*(For now the storm was close above them) struck,*
*Furrowing a giant oak, and javelining*
*With darted spikes and splinters of the wood*
*The dark earth round. . . .*

(Merlin and Vivien.)

*. . . the spring, that down,*
*From underneath a plume of lady-fern,*
*Sang, and the sand danced at the bottom of it*

(Balin and Balan.)

*. . . the spires*
*Prick'd with incredible pinnacles into heaven.*

(The Holy Grail.)

*The long low dune, and lazy-plunging sea.*

(The Last Tournament.)

*Whereat the novice, crying with clasp'd hands*
*Shame on her own garrulity garrulously. . . .*

(Guinevere.)

*Dry clash'd his harness in the icy caves*
*And barren chasms, and all to left and right*
*The bare black cliff clang'd round him, as he based*
*His feet on juts of slippery crag that rang*
*Sharp-smitten with the dint of armed heels—*
*And on a sudden, lo! the level lake,*
*And the long glories of the winter moon.*

(The Passing of Arthur.)

It is easy for an analysis, like that which I have attempted, to give the impression that poets act by rule and precedent, with their tables loaded with text-books on prosody and their heads full of trochees and anapaests. That, of course, is very far from the truth. A great poet's mind is stored with the rhythms of nature and art and, as he broods over his subject, he evolves rhythmic forms to suit it. Great poets may now and then set about deliberate experiments, as Tennyson and Bridges did in their imitations of classical metres, but such attempts are exceptional. As a rule, the greater the poet the greater will be the freedom and variety of his attack. In attempting to analyse the result it is impossible to avoid giving impressions of too great regularity and precision. Nevertheless, I think such an attempt may help to a fuller understanding of a poet's work, although analysis can never fully enable anyone else to emulate it. A great artist achieves his results by subtle and instinctive combinations of rhythm, vowel sound, assonance and alliteration, but these are further coloured by the meaning and emotions of the poem and the mental associations of the words used, so that the same rhythm may have very different implications in different contexts. An amusing example of this is given in Hallam Tennyson's *Memoir* of the poet (single volume edition, pp. 394 and 395.) Tennyson's friend, Coventry Patmore, had written an article in which he referred to the six-syllable iambic as the most solemn of English metres, and said that if one iambic were added, making it an eight-syllable measure, it immediately became 'the most joyous and high-spirited' of our metres.

To this Tennyson replied as follows:

'My dear C. P.,

*Specimen of the "most solemn" English metre:*

*How glad am I to walk*
*With Susan on the shore!*
*How glad am I to talk!*
*I kiss her o'er and o'er.*
*I clasp her slender waist,*
*We kiss, we are so fond.*
*When she and I are thus embraced*
*There's not a joy beyond.*

Is this C. P.'s most solemn?

*Specimen of "the most high-spirited metre".*

> *How strange it is, O God, to wake,*
> *To watch and wake while others sleep,*
> *Till heart and sight and hearing ache*
> *For common objects that would keep*
>
> *Our awful inner ghostly sense*
> *Unroused, lest it should chance to mark*
> *The life that haunts the emptiness*
> *And horrors of the dark.*

Is this C. P.'s most rapid and high-spirited?

A. T.'

V

# *Some MSS. of the 'Idylls of the King' and a Note on Tennyson as a Narrative Poet*

EARLY MSS. of Tennyson's *Idylls of the King* throw valuable light on his methods of composition in his most ambitious work, begun between his fortieth and fiftieth years, when his technical skill was at its zenith, and elaborated with such thoroughness and patience that the last poem of the series was not published till twenty-six years after the first. Moreover, these MSS. contain some fine lines and passages which Tennyson, for one reason or another, ultimately discarded, and I think these should be preserved.

The following notes are based on a series of thin quarto note-books of blue unruled paper with marbled covers and red leather backs, which were bound for the poet by his wife, and one large vellum-bound book, some fifteen inches by six inches in size, of the type described by Edward FitzGerald as 'Butcher's Books'.[1]

The poet disapproved of the publication of variorum readings and other 'chips of the workshop' as he called them; and it is inevitable from the nature of the subject that my notes should be somewhat fragmentary; but I have tried to avoid the inclusion of anything which could be regarded as 'chips' and to confine myself to quotations of real substance.

The *Idylls* are referred to in the order of their publication, not in that of their appearance in the collection as ultimately printed.

### *Geraint and Enid*

The MS. of 'Enid' (published in 1859), which was the first title of the Idyll afterwards divided into 'The Marriage of Geraint'

[1] See *Idylls of the King* in the Eversley Edition of Tennyson's Works, p. 468. In T. J. Wise's Bibliography of Tennyson, Vol. I (printed for private circulation in 1908), are included some interesting excerpts from MSS. and Trial Books of 'The Coming of Arthur', 'Pelleas and Ettarre' and 'The Passing of Arthur'.

and 'Geraint and Enid', has all the appearance of a first draft. It consists of a considerable number of separate passages (in all about 750 lines) covering the whole scope of the story and almost all very hastily written and scattered about the book without any proper sequence. Some passages are written crosswise, some lengthwise on the page; some forward through the book, some backwards, and all mingled together in complete disorder.

There is another notebook, unbound, but of similar paper and size, which contains fragments of these Idylls. It appears to be contemporaneous with, and complementary to, the first book, and the contents of the two dovetail into one another more or less consistently. The second, also, is clearly a first draft. Its most interesting passage is a version of Enid's song, which contains some excellent lines.

### *Enid's Song*

*Come in, the ford is roaring on the plain,*
*The distant hills are pale across the rain;*
*Come in, come in, for open is the gate.*
*Come in, poor man, and let the tempest blow.*
*Let fortune frown and old possession go,*
*But health is wealth in high or low estate;*
*Tho' fortune frown thou shalt not hear us rail,*
*The frown of fortune never turn'd us pale,*
*For man is man and master of his Fate.*
*Turn, Fortune, turn thy wheel with smile or frown,*
*With thy false wheel we go not up or down,*
*Our hoard is little but our hearts are great.*
*Smile and we smile, the lords of many lands,*
*Frown and we smile, the lords of our own hands,*
*For man is man and master of his Fate.*
*The river ford will fall on yonder plain,*
*The flying rainbow chase the flying rain,*
*The sun at last will smile however late;*
*Come in, come in, whoever lingers there*
*Nor scorn the ruin'd house and homely fare,*
*The house is poor but open is the gate.*

The interest of these two books is very fragmentary.

There are one or two good phrases used to indicate the passage of time—always a difficulty in narrative verse, unless the poet is prepared to adopt the Homeric device of frank repetition.

Here are two examples never actually used in the published Idylls. The first is for dawn:

*But when the third day from the hunting morn*
*Beneath the swelling bosom of the cloud*
*Had cast her golden zone along the dark. . . .*

The second for evening:

*But when the oak became*
*Thrice shorter than his shadow. . . .*

Here is a poetic version of an idea of Malory's which Tennyson never printed:

*Then spake King Arthur, inasmuch as I,*
*When first we founded our fair Table Round*
*With Merlin's aid and counsel thereunto,*
*To be an image of the mighty world,*
*Made oath before the Lord of Heaven and Earth*
*That we would never set ourselves to meat*
*Before the witnessing some noble deed*
*Or hearing one told nobly. . . .*

In Malory it is merely stated that the King would never sit down to meat on the feast of Pentecost until he had witnessed some adventure. Tennyson, characteristically, ennobles Malory's idea.

The notebooks give many examples of the skilful improvements by which Tennyson was often able to make a good line or passage astonishingly better.

For example, the MS. has these lines:

*Then Enid answered, harder to be moved*
*Than hardest rulers in their day of power,*
*With ancient injuries unavenged, and said:*
*'In this poor gown, etc.'*

In the published version this becomes:

*But Enid answered, harder to be moved*
*Than hardest tyrants in their day of power,*
*With lifelong injuries burning unavenged,*
*And now their hour is come, and Enid said:*
*'In this poor gown. . . .'*

But for the most part the passages included in this rough draft show only very minor differences from the final form. For instance, the following lines, amongst many others, which have very bold rhythmical and verbal devices, occur in the rough draft and also in the published poems.

*As slopes a brook above a little stone*
*Running too violently to break upon it . . .*

*The hot hiss*
*And bustling whistle of the squire who scoured*
*His master's armour . . .*

*His charger trampling many a prickly star*
*Of sprouted thistle in the broken stones.*

*The sound of many a heavily galloping hoof*
*Broke on her ear, and turning round she saw*
*Dust, and the points of lances bicker in it.*

*And at a sudden swerving of the road,*
*Tho' happpily down on a bank of grass,*
*The prince, without a word, from his horse fell.*

*Evermore*
*Seem'd catching at a rootless thorn, and then*
*Went slipping down horrible precipices,*
*And wildly striking out her limbs, awoke.*

The famous nightingale passage also occurs here in MS. almost in its final form.

### *Guinevere*

This Idyll (first published 1859) was begun on July 9, 1857, when Tennyson brought his wife—'as a birthday present'—the first lines of the poem which he had made and on which the whole was afterwards founded.

> *But hither shall I never come again,*
> *Never lie by thy side; see thee no more—*
> *Farewell!*[1]

It was finished in January 1858 though the final touches were not given till March 15 of that year.

What appears to be the first draft of the poem is included in one of the marbled quarto notebooks, the first part of which contains fragments of the Idyll extending beyond the point at which these lines occur in the published poem.

Oddly enough, the lines are not included in this draft, though they do occur in a revised draft of Arthur's speech and Guinevere's lament, which immediately follows. This is, I think, characteristic. Tennyson probably omitted the passage from the first draft because the lines were so firmly imprinted in his memory that it was not necessary to include them in the draft which was really in the nature of an aide-memoire.

The first draft consists of fragments beginning with what was apparently intended to be the commencement of the poem, a description of Guinevere's ride to Amesbury. In the published Idyll this description is preceded by an account of Lancelot's last visit to the Queen and his detection by Modred.

The notebook version begins with these fine lines, which Tennyson afterwards omitted—probably because he was not satisfied with the word 'flare'.

> *So fled the sad Queen through the moony night*
> *In which no moon appeared, but one vast flare*
> *Of all the heavens, moon-white from verge to verge.*

This is followed by a number of fragments of varying length more or less in the sequence of the poem, but intersperséd with

[1] Lady Tennyson's diary—quoted in Hallam Tennyson's *Memoir*, p. 353.

a great many blank pages, left, no doubt, that the poet might fill in intervening passages if he wished to do so. Some of these fragments are carefully—but most of them roughly—written. Here and there are passages which find no place in the completed Idyll. For example, on one page occurs this isolated fragment:

*Ah, noble heart,*
*Ah, flower of kindliness and courtesy,*
*To take the shame and horror to thyself*
*When I betrayed thee. . . .*

Later come these lines:

*I could not worship him, that God in man,*
*I dared not, as I dare not worship God*
*. . . and yet am I forgiven—forgiven!*

Both passages were no doubt intended for Guinevere's lament after Arthur has left her.

Mention may also be made of one interesting variation, which makes rather more clear the point of a passage in the final text.

*Yet not less, Guinevere,*
*For I was ever virgin save for thee,*
*My love through flesh hath wrought into thy life*
*So that I must pronounce I love thee still.*
This is the meed of my part maidenhood
*To love thee still though false—so let it be.*
*Let no man doubt the folly of the King*
*Nor doubt that like a child he loves her still.*

The line in Roman type makes clear the point in the first part of the text, but Tennyson was probably dissatisfied with the rather obscure phrase 'part maidenhood'. The concluding lines were also omitted from the final version, the poet probably thinking them too bitter and self-depreciatory for the King's lips at this crisis.

A characteristic of this fragmentary first draft is the number of rough notes, often mere indications of the rhythm and wording of the final text, which are jotted down here and there, apparently just to fix an idea which had come into the poet's mind. This hardly occurs in other MSS. which contain, generally speaking, only completed passages whether in verse or prose.

This draft is immediately followed by a revised draft of the King's farewell speech and departure and Guinevere's lament, and the rest of the book, which probably carried the poem to its conclusion, is torn out.

A revised draft of some of the earlier part of this Idyll is found in the 'Butcher's Book'. This begins with the first speech of the little maid and continues to the end of her last long speech.

*Till he by miracle was approven King.*

The draft is a fair copy, but varying in many unimportant points from the final text.

It is perhaps worth mentioning that here Tennyson uses Malory's name 'Dundagil' for the more melodious 'Tintagil' which he afterwards adopted.

Another interesting variant is in the description of the spirits of the hills. The draft has

*With all their hair blown back like cyclamen*

where the final text says:

*With all their dewy hair blown back like flame.*

## *The Holy Grail*

Tennyson hesitated long before embarking on the Grail subject, as he feared that it could hardly be handled without incurring a charge of irreverence. When once he set about it, however, the poem came like a breath of inspiration and was finished in a few days.

The MS. clearly bears this out. What appears to be the first draft of the poem occurs in one of the marbled notebooks. This begins with a prose version, which follows almost exactly the course of the published poem. It is well written, and very little corrected, and runs, with one or two brief lapses into verse, right up to the point where Lancelot, after his madness, embarks in the little boat. His voyage to the enchanted castle and adventure there are then treated fully in verse, and the King's speech follows, the first part in prose and the end in verse. The prose sketch is immediately followed by a fairly complete draft of the whole poem in verse. This is written in a good hand straight through on the right-hand pages of the book, but not carefully enough to be a fair copy. Occasionally a passage is interpolated on the left-hand page. There is a break where Galahad is first mentioned by Percivale, a page being left blank and then fragments of verse written in very roughly. Another break occurs at Percivale's description of Arthur's great hall, a blank being left for seven lines which are to be found written in verse in the prose version and which Tennyson (doubtless to save himself the fatigue of copying) left to be filled in afterwards. The same thing occurs later, when the rebuke of the hermit, 'O son, thou hast not true humility', and the twelve following lines, which had been interpolated in the prose version, are omitted.

The verse draft runs on continuously to the end of the poem, but with two important omissions; first, Ambrosius's interruption (bottom of p. 299 in the Eversley volume) and Percivale's Confession which follows it. This episode occurs in the prose version, where it is added on the left-hand pages, part of it being written roughly in verse. The other omitted episode is written in prose on the left-hand pages as an interpolation in the verse draft. This is the tale of Sir Bors. It is written rather roughly and gets no further than the point where Bors first encounters the pagan tribe. Then follow a few scattered lines of verse and prose:

*By whom the blood beats and the blossom blows*
*And the sea rolls. . . .*

. . . . .

'And it would never be well for this Britain till the Christ were put down and the sun-worship put up again.'

Then some of the lines describing the vision of Sir Bors, very roughly scribbled and with a somewhat mysterious opening word:

*wicker work*
*The seven cold stars of Arthur's wain,*
*. . . and in a moment all across*
*The seven cold stars, in colour like a hand*
*Before a burning taper, past the Grail,*
*. . . and through the cleft*
*I saw the torn sky and the flying rack.*

The prose sketch is a particularly good one, written in a style which is at once vivid, rich and simple and quite unlike that of Malory, while the story moves swiftly and logically forward and the imaginative atmosphere is admirably maintained. The following extract, describing the end of Galahad's quest, will give a good idea of the whole, and a comparison with the corresponding passage in the completed Idyll shows how skilfully the poet elaborated into verse this first embodiment of his thought.

The passage runs as follows:

> '. . . and he leapt into the boat and I was alone for I could not follow. And the boat went with an exceeding swiftness and thrice over him the Heavens opened and blazed with thunder like the shouting of all the sons of God. And when first they opened I beheld him far out on the great sea and over his head was the holy vessel clothed in white samite or a luminous cloud. And when they blazed I beheld him very far away and over him the holy vessel redder than any rose whereby I knew that the veil had been withdrawn from it: and when the Heavens opened and blazed the third time I saw him no bigger than the point over an i and far away behind him in a clear spot of sky I saw the gates of the spiritual city no larger than a pearl and over it a tiny blood-red spark[?] and dwelt there and I knew it was the Holy Grail. Then the Heavens came down as tho' they would drown the world and I saw no more.'

The completed poem, of course, adds many beauties of detail to the prose draft, as, for example, in the description of the Knights passing through the narrow streets of Camelot out upon their Quest (*Works*, p. 424); while the final version gains greatly by the addition, at the beginning, of the description of Percivale's friendship with Ambrosius and their first conversation about the Grail.

Many of the fragments of verse inserted in the prose sketch are probably in the nature of key lines which formed the basis of the poem in Tennyson's mind, e.g. the lines, which are taken almost word for word from Malory:

> *I saw the fiery face as of a child*
> *Which smote itself into the bread and went.*

And Galahad's cry:

> *'But I, Sir Arthur, saw the Holy Grail,*
> *I saw the Holy Grail and heard a cry*
> *"O Galahad and O Galahad follow me".'*

An interesting point about these lines is that here only in all the Idylls is the King addressed as '*Sir* Arthur', showing that Galahad, as the chosen Knight, feels himself the King's equal and independent of earthly titles.

The verse draft contains very few lines that do not occur in the completed poem, though of course many lines were substantially altered.

King Arthur uses one telling line to describe the mirage which his Knights are pursuing in place of their plain duty of 'rightful strength redressing human wrong'. Instead of this, he says, they are following:

> *A sound, a luminous cloud, a holy nun.*

Tennyson probably thought this too slighting a description of the Quest to put into the King's mouth and he afterwards omitted the line.

Lancelot, in describing his madness, speaks of his defeat at the hands of

> *Mean knights, to whom the ventage of my sword*
> *And shadow of my spear had been enow*
> *To scare them from me once.*

The curious, but effective, word 'ventage' disappears from the final text.

There are, of course, countless alterations which strikingly improve the text—one or two may perhaps be quoted.

A famous passage begins in this first draft:

> *There rose a hill that none but man could climb,*
> *Scarred with ten thousand wintry water-courses.*

This is enormously improved by the substitution of 'a hundred' for 'ten thousand', though it is hard to say why.

Again the line

> *He saw some little of this wonder too.*

is greatly improved by a simple transposition.

*Some little of this wonder he too saw.*

Another good example is the following from the first draft:

*Beheld*
*A castle like a rock upon a rock,*
*With chasm-like portals open to the sea.*

One added line makes a world of difference here:

*and looking up,*
*Behold, the enchanted towers of Carbonek,*
*A castle like a rock upon a rock*
*With chasm-like portals open to the sea.*

But, speaking generally, except for minor alterations, the verse has already attained practically its final form. The structure of the verse paragraphs is the same as in the finished Idyll, and so are many of the most striking rhythms such as:

*And high at top a city wall'd: the spires*
*Prick'd with incredible pinnacles into heaven.*

*and even as he spoke,*
*In silver armour Galahad suddenly shone*
*Before us. . . .*

### *The Coming and Passing of Arthur*

In one of the marbled notebooks, unfortunately much mutilated, are some of Tennyson's first thoughts for these two Idylls, which were published in 1869—'The Passing' being made up of the 'Morte d'Arthur' from the volume of 1842, with lines added at the beginning and end. The fragments in this book are both in verse and prose.

The following passages suggest that the poet originally intended to deal fully in 'The Coming' with Arthur's battles against the heathen and the rebel kings and lords.

*Ulfius and Brastias and Bedivere*
*Smote down the rebel lords and men-at-arms,*
*And Arthur smote not his own lords, but made*
*Still for the kings, and by main might smote down*

*The King Brandagoras of Latangor*
*And Anguisant of Ireland, Morganore*
*And Lot of Orkney. . . .*

The poet must have been sorry to sacrifice this resounding battery of names and titles, and also the grim humour of this passage:

*From whereout*
*A stalwart savage, chieftain of the horde,*
*Strode mocking 'art thou come to eat me lad?'*
*Said Arthur 'Thou hast eaten up the land.'*
*'And thee too now, sir stripling, will I eat.'*
*'But thee the worms' said Arthur, and with might*
*Smote him and after deadly contest slew,*
*Then falling on the host, they fled: he drove*
*The heathen and he kill'd the beast and fell'd*
*The forest letting in the sun. . . .*

The following verse sketch of a dialogue between Bedivere and Arthur is also worth quoting. It was of course intended for the beginning of 'The Passing':

*This heard the bold Sir Bedivere and passed*
*Within the tent and spake 'My Lord, the King,*
*I find a feeble whiteness as of dawn*
*In the far East. . . .*
*Wilt thou not rise and follow to the west*
*And . . .*
*That all the sooner we may turn again*
*And see the sunrise light the golden wings*
*That Merlin gave thine image on the Hall.'*
*Then spake King Arthur*
*'O think'st thou we shall ever turn again*
*To light and sunrise in the golden East?*
*We follow night and sunset in the West*
*And those who love the King will die with me.'*
*And therewithal return'd on Bedivere*
*The burden of a hymn himself had sung.*
*He clash'd his arms together and he said*
*. . . 'King art thou in East and West,*
*Strike for the King and die: let the King reign!'*

The following is a prose sketch for Arthur's speech at the commencement of 'The Passing':

> O me, but this fight is far other
> than those wherein we drove the heathen
> from the West or the Roman wall.
> I fight against my people and the Knights
> whom I have made, and that is to me
> even as mine own death.
> That sweet smile which Guinevere and Lancelot
> smiled in the May woods was cruel as many
> deaths.
> They say that I am no king: they know not,
> Nor do I myself, whence I came.
> Theirs is the blame who fostered me and
> spoke softly to me and held me sacred and
> drest me delicately nor ever let a foul
> word be spoken before me and shewed me
> the fields and hills and said 'this is thy
> realm for ever'. They told me that I was
> a King's son, but that I should not
> see my father on earth and I believed them
> and believe them still.

The last half of this interesting passage possibly reflects a mood of the poet himself in moments when he felt himself cut off from his kind, partly by his upbringing in the secluded and studious atmosphere of Somersby, partly by his sensitiveness and habit of introspection and that sense, which was always with him, of his poetic mission.

## *Gareth and Lynette*

Tennyson said that this poem gave him more trouble than anything else he ever wrote except perhaps 'Aylmer's Field', as he found the short 'snip-snap of conversation' so difficult to deal with in narrative form.

The notebook in which the MS. is written begins with a prose sketch which takes the story to the point where Gareth leaves Camelot after Lynette upon the quest which the King has given him. This sketch embodies a subsidiary story which Tennyson afterwards discarded. It is contained in the opening paragraphs.

> 'Lot's wife Bellicent, the Queen of Orkney, sat in her castle on the sea and she was lost in thought, for there had come to her a noise that Queen Guinevere was false with Lancelot: and thereupon the Queen who had long been haunted by a passion for Sir Lamorack, had yielded herself to him and thus dishonoured her house. But now she said to herself "Lo if Guinevere have not sinned and this rumour is untrue, I shall be the first woman to have broken the fair order of the Table Round and made a Knight forego his vows and so my name shall go down thro' the world for ever: but if Guinevere have sinned, then the sin will be hers and my shame covered by her shame."'

Then when Bellicent's son Gareth asks her for leave to go to Arthur's Court and be made knight, she makes him, as the condition of her consent, take a vow to seek into this scandal and bring her word whether it be true.

> '"But think not", she says, "to ask this of the knights for they hold together by their vows and are sworn to speak no slander and from them wilt thou learn nothing, but thou shalt mingle with the thralls of the house and with those that hand the dish across the bar, for these are they that know the things of a house and delight in the evils thereof and from them shalt thou learn and bring back the truth of this matter to me thy mother: for it were shame that another should be shamed by his own Queen not knowing, moreover this sin will pass thro' all the Table Round and ruin the King's purpose if it be not put an end to."'

This episode is not found in Malory, who gives no explanation at all of Gareth's odd whim of being made a thrall in Arthur's kitchen. Malory, indeed, describes Queen Bellicent as much incensed with Arthur when she discovers what has happened to her son. Tennyson afterwards abandoned the story of Bellicent's infidelity and made her lay this condition of thralldom on her son, merely because she thought that he would revolt from it and therefore would not leave her for Arthur's Court.

This prose sketch, like that for 'The Holy Grail', is written in a good clear hand and without corrections. It contains the description of the approach of Gareth and his two men to the mystic city of Camelot, and the conversation with the old seer (here called Merlin) at the city gate, none of which occurs in Malory. It does not, however, contain the description (found in the finished Idyll) of the various supplicants and Mark's messenger coming to Arthur in the Hall, while Gareth is waiting to ask his boon.

After this prose fragment comes the first verse draft of the poem. This goes up to and includes the description of Gareth's vassalage—not quite so far as the prose sketch: the verse is fairly continuous, but a good deal is interpolated on the left-hand pages and occasionally a fragment is written in prose. The dialogue with Mark's messenger evidently suggested to Tennyson the theme of 'The Last Tournament', which was written immediately after Gareth and published in the same volume, for a prose outline of a projected beginning of this Idyll is interpolated in the Gareth story. This outline brings in the story of Bellicent and Lamorack already mentioned. The fragment, which is not reproduced in the published *Idylls*, runs as follows:

'Sir Dagonet, the King's fool, stood before the hall of Arthur and the wind was blowing and the leaves flying in the woods below.

'And below him riding three abreast there past into the wood Sir Gawain, Sir Modred and Sir Gaheris: and the face of Gawain was red as tho' with wine; and the face of Modred was white but he had bitten his thin lips and they were bloody: and so they past away.

'And about an hour after there rode into the wood Sir Lamorack and his head was down and his heart darkened for his old love Bellicent was dead.

'And the dwarf skipped upon the steps before the hall and out of the hall came Tristram and cried to him:

'"O fool, why skippest thou?"

and the dwarf pointed to the wood and said:

"They are gone to keep the vows of the King."

and Tristram said: "Who are gone?" and he answered, "The sons of the Queen; for Lancelot has kept the vows of the King and thou also: for ye have all lain by Queens so that no King knoweth his own son."'

Up to this point the MS. gives no evidence that the Gareth story was causing the poet any exceptional difficulty. The poem is followed through its natural sequence and the verse appears to have been written with reasonable ease, except that there is rather more interpolation on the left-hand page than, for example, occurs in the 'Grail' MS.

In the 'Butcher's Book' in which the draft is continued, the condition is very different.

The Gareth fragments in this book are written rapidly in a rough hand without correction, and dotted about the book in the wildest confusion.

This irregularity of composition is probably due to the difficulty which the poet experienced in dealing with this part of the story, which is largely conversational.

This meant that the flow of composition was frequently interrupted, and Tennyson seems to have opened the book more or less at random and jotted down passages, generally of short length, as they occurred to him, without concerning himself as to the sequence of his text.

One would hardly think this a way to make a difficult task easier, but Tennyson had a remarkable power of retaining his verse in his memory, and it is probable that when he came to write out the next draft, he did so with very little reference to what he had already written.

In so very rough and imperfect a text one would expect to find many variations from the final version, but little deserving quotation. There are, however, one or two points of interest. For instance, the draft has these lines:

*And the live green had kindled into flowers*
*For it was nigh the feast of Pentecost.*

For the second line the published version has:

*For it was past the time of Easterday.*

a more melodious line and conveying a much more genial suggestion.

Sometimes an alteration calls attention to the aptness and effectiveness of an unusual word.

Thus the MS. in describing the carvings of the mystic gate at Camelot, refers to

*The dragons' tails and elvish emblemings.*

The final version has:

*The dragon-boughts and elvish emblemings.*

the word 'bought' being apparently remembered from Spenser's '*Faerie Queene*, Bk. I, Canto XI, Ver. xi.

### *Balin and Balan*

Tennyson evidently gave a great deal of thought to this Idyll and tried several arrangements of certain incidents of the story, which was mostly original, with only a small foundation in Malory. Hallam Tennyson quotes in full (Eversley Edn., pp. 425–432) a prose version, entitled 'The Dolorous Stroke' (a phrase of Malory's not used in the published Idyll), which the poet is said to have dictated to Sir James Knowles almost without a pause. From the existing MSS. of the Idyll, to which I shall presently refer in detail, it seems probable that this prose version was the crystallization of a long preliminary study of the material. It is a remarkably finished and clean piece of writing, which the published poem follows fairly closely, though this omits the close of the prose sketch,

> 'Then when the damsel left them, came the Lady of the Lake and found Sir Balin and Sir Balan at their last breaths and caused them to be interred and sang above them an high song.'

It is characteristic of Tennyson's self-discipline that he jettisoned this fine passage, no doubt feeling that the introduction of the Lady of the Lake would divert interest from the main theme of the poem. He preferred to concentrate on the main theme and therefore closed with the beautiful farewell of Balan to his dying brother whom he has unwittingly slain:

*'Good-bye, true brother, here. Good-morrow, there.'*

The reference to the Lady of the Lake is not taken from Malory. Indeed, in his version of the story, the Lady is beheaded by Balin very early in its development.

MS. fragments of this Idyll are contained in two of the marbled notebooks (quarto) and in the large 'Butcher's Book' already mentioned: they present all the appearance of a first draft, consisting as they do of disconnected verse passages, scattered about more or less inconsequently, and tentative prose sketches. They seem, therefore, to represent Tennyson's first thoughts about this Idyll and to have been written before the composition of the prose sketch dictated to Knowles.

The most interesting thing about these MS. fragments is that in them one can see the poet making use of his last opportunity to weave some thread of continuous story through the episodic structure of the Idylls. The following list shows the dates of publication and final place in the series of the various Idylls:

| | | |
|---|---|---|
| 1859. | The Geraint Idylls . . . . | 3 and 4 |
| | Merlin and Vivien . . . . . | 6 |
| | Lancelot and Elaine . . . . . | 7 |
| | Guinevere . . . . . . | 11 |

These four stories are quite independent and have no connexion with one another.

| | | |
|---|---|---|
| 1869. | Coming of Arthur . . . . . . | 1 |
| | Holy Grail . . . . . . | 8 |
| | Pelleas and Ettarre . . . . . . | 9 |
| | Passing of Arthur . . . . . . | 12 |

These four are also independent, though the 'Passing' follows logically on 'Guinevere'.

| | | |
|---|---|---|
| 1872. | Gareth and Lynette . . . . . . | 2 |
| | The Last Tournament . . . . | 10 |
| 1885. | Balin and Balan . . . . . . | 5 |

'Balin and Balan', though not published till thirteen years after 'Gareth and Lynette', was written soon after it. These two Idylls and 'The Last Tournament' should therefore be considered together. In them Tennyson introduced, for the first time, the sinister figure of King Mark of Cornwall. He appears first in 'Gareth and Lynette' as a Vassal King who sends a messenger with a present to Arthur's Court, asking to be made a member of the

Round Table. Arthur rejects the gift and sends back the messenger, cursing Mark as

*Craven, a man of plots,*
*Craft, poisonous counsels, wayside ambushings.*

The Gareth Idyll was ultimately placed second in the series and Mark's hostility and treachery are therefore very early emphasized. He next appears in 'Balin and Balan' (placed fifth of the series) where Vivien, coming upon Balin in the forest, is described as 'a damsel errant from the Hall of Mark'. She inflames Balin's fury with tales of the Queen's infidelity and thus, though unintentionally, leads to the fight and death of Balin and his brother Balan.

The next reference to Mark is at the beginning of the sixth Idyll, 'Merlin and Vivien', where Mark and Vivien are shown in the former's palace at Tintagil, conspiring against Arthur, as a result of which Vivien goes to Camelot and by the use of a spell binds in an eternal trance the wizard Merlin, the chief of Arthur's Counsellors, thus striking a deadly blow at the King's rule.

The last appearance of Mark occurs in 'The Last Tournament', published with 'Gareth and Lynette' in 1872 and placed tenth in the series immediately before 'Guinevere' and 'The Passing', which describes the final catastrophe. This Idyll shows Tristram, the second mightiest knight of Arthur's Court, going straight from victory at the 'Tournament of the dead Innocence' at Camelot, to make love to Mark's Queen, Iseult, at Tintagil, where he is treacherously slain by Mark.

In the 'Balin and Balan' MSS. can be seen the piecing together of the central part of this Mark sequence.

In one of the marbled notebooks (which I will call 'A') occurs this interesting prose sketch:

'Pellam the King who held and lost with Lot, had his realm render'd tributary, and he had no child, but Sir Garlon, his heir, was his nephew, and Sir Garlon hated King Arthur because the King had refused to make him of his Round Table, knowing him, and many times in his anger he had sworn that, come what might come, he would pay the tribute no more. And it chanced on a time that he sat drinking red wine in Lyonesse with King Mark, for these were close friends: and they spoke of the great King, who hoped to bring the world right by swearing his knights to vows of perfect obedience and perfect purity: and either laugh'd and scorned at the phantasy of so many mighty knights being pure.

'And there was with him a damsel of that Court who bewitched men with her beauty, and she said "what wilt thou wager, Sir King, with me that I do not go to the Court of this (illegible) and bring back love tokens of these pure ones, yea even were it a curl from the golden beard of Arthur. Have we not heard that this Lancelot worships no unwedded damsel but the Queen herself, to shew forsooth, his utter selflessness, swears by her, and fights in her name? Here be snakes in the grass, which methinks I can stir till they sting."

'"Go when thou wilt," said Mark, "and an thou canst make a mischief among them, there is nothing I will not give thee." Then spake Sir Garlon, "I ride on the morrow back to the castle of King Pellam on the way to Arthur. Ride thou with me." And she took with her a squire whom now she treated as a lover and now she mock'd as child. And the boy was besotted with her. But King Pellam thrust her from the gates and there she dwelt among the woods awhile, waiting for Sir Garlon to go with her, and Garlon ever kept the Tribute from being paid.'

Here the fragment ends, but it was evidently followed by a description of Vivien's encounter with Balan in the forest and the disastrous fight of the two brothers. The story is continued in another of the marbled books ('B'), which seems once to have contained a complete draft of the poem, whether written before or after the prose sketch is uncertain, but clearly anterior to the Knowles prose version. The early part of the notebook is mostly torn out, but near the end comes the following passage, which describes Vivien's journey to Camelot after the death of the brothers, with Balin's shield and locks of both the brothers' hair, which she has cut off.

*Stealthily sped she then to Arthur's hall,*
*Took the dead hair, and the besotted boy*
*And battered shield, and came before the Queen;*
*Knelt lowly then, and bidden rise arose,*
*And stood with folded hands and downward eyes*
*Of glancing corner and all meekly said—*

*'My father died in battle for thy King,*
*My mother on his body in open field*
*Brake her true heart. An orphan maid am I,*
*For what small share of beauty may be mine*
*Pursued by Mark the King; yea—and by one*
*Sir Tristram—of the Table—nay perchance*
*I wrong him, being fearful, full of shame;*
*The Cornish manners be so rough; but lo,*
*I bring thee here a message from the dead.'*
*And therewithal showing Sir Balan's hair*
*'Know ye not this? not so, belike; but this*
*A most strange red, is easier known.' The Queen*
*Took the dead hair and slightly shuddering ask'd*
*'Sir Balin's? is he slain?' 'Yea, noble Queen,*
*Likewise his brother Balan: for they fought,*
*Not knowing—some misprision of their shields—*
*I know not what. I found them side by side*
*And wounded to the death, unlac'd their helms,*
*And gave them air and water, held their heads,*
*Wept with them; and this Balin joy'd my heart*
*Calling thee stainless wife and perfect Queen*
*Heaven's white earth-angel; then they bad me clip*
*One tress from either head and bring it thee,*
*Proof that my message is not feigned; and prayed*
*King Arthur would despatch some holy man,*
*As these had lain together in one womb,*
*To give them burial in a single grave—*
*Sent their last blessings to the King and thee,*
*And therewithal their dying word, that thou,*
*For that good service I had done thy knights,*
*Wouldst yield me shelter for mine innocency.'*
*To whom the Queen made answer 'we must hear*
*Thy story further; thou shalt bide the while.*
*I know no more of thee than that thy tale*
*Hath chilled me to the heart. Ghastly mischance,*
*Enough to make all childless motherhood*
*Fain so to bide for ever. Where do they lie?'*
*And Vivien's voice was broken answering her.*
*'Dead in a nameless corner of the woods*

*Each lock'd in either's arms. I know the place,*
*But scarce can word it plain for thee to know.'*
*'And therefore damsel shalt thou ride at once*
*With Arthur's knights and guide them thro' the woods.*
*Thy wish, and these dead men's, if such were theirs,*
*Must bide mine answer till we meet again.'*
*After, when Vivien on returning came*
*To Guinevere and spake 'I saw the twain*
*Buried, and wept above their woodland grave.*
*But grant me now my wish and theirs,' the Queen*
*All glittering like may sunshine among leaves*
*In green and gold, and plumed with green, replied:*
*'A moiety of thy tale is proven true;*
*Yet must we test thee more; but even now*
*We ride an-hawking with Sir Lancelot.*
*He hath given me a fair falcon which he train'd.*
*We go to fly her. Bide thou here the while.'*
*But when she rode with Lancelot down the plain*
*Their talk was all of training, terms of Art,*
*Feeding and diet, jesses, leash and lure.*
*'She is too noble' he said 'to check at pies*
*Nor will she rake: there is no baseness in her.'*
*Here when the Queen demanded as by chance*
*'Know ye this stranger woman?' 'Let her be'*
*Said Lancelot, and unhooded casting from him*
*The goodly falcon loose; she tower'd; her bells*
*Tone under tone, shrilled; and they lifted up*
*Their eager faces, wondering at the strength*
*Boldness and royal knighthood of the bird*
*Who pounced her quarry and slew it many a time.*
*They rode; and half forgotten of the Queen*
*Among her maidens broidering Vivien sat*
*And whisper'd.*

In the published poem this episode, including the conspiracy at Mark's palace, Vivien's encounter with the brothers in the wood and her sojourn at King Arthur's Court, is split up and distributed between two Idylls—'Balin and Balan' and 'Merlin and Vivien'. In the former Idyll, which comes first, Vivien is described as wandering in the forest 'a damsel errant from the Court of Mark', with her page. She meets Balin and maddens him with scandal about Lancelot and the Queen. Her visit to Pellam's castle, rejection by him and dalliance with Carlon in the wood, are described afterwards by Balan to his dying brother.

The story of Vivien's offer to seduce the Knights of the Round Table, which comes at the beginning of the prose sketch (Notebook 'A'), is told in 'Merlin and Vivien', which comes later in the series. It is followed by Vivien's journey to Arthur's Court, her interview with Guinevere, the hawking episode, and her intrigues with the Knights. The whole is now quite unconnected with 'Balin and Balan' and therefore differs considerably from the verse narrative quoted above (from 'B'). There is, however, in another notebook ('C') a draft in verse of this part of the sequence, more or less in the form in which it was actually used in 'Merlin and Vivien'.

This Idyll was published twenty-six years before 'Balin and Balan' (which appeared in the Demeter volume of 1885 and is there called 'An Introduction to "Merlin and Vivien"') and thirteen years before that poem was written. This particular episode was therefore not included in the early published editions of 'Merlin and Vivien', appearing for the first time in 1874.

It is curious to find Tennyson first constructing this continuous story and then breaking it up and distributing it about two separate Idylls. I think the reason for this was that he feared by the introduction of too definite a thread of narrative, to interfere with the episodic form, which he had deliberately chosen as best suited to the subject and his own powers. In the published poem, therefore, the Mark story is introduced intermittently and almost incidentally, but this is managed so skilfully that the sequence of events is brought quite clearly before the reader. I think that critics are apt to overlook the effectiveness of the idyllic form which Tennyson deliberately chose and the skill with which he employed it.

Before leaving the 'Balin and Balan' MSS. I will mention a few interesting passages omitted or varying from the published *Idylls*.

In the 'B' notebook these lines occur in the description of Guinevere's encounter with Lancelot in the Palace garden. The Queen is contrasting the roses and lilies which are blooming at her side (Eversley, p. 168):

*'Better,' she said, 'I love this garden rose*
*Deep-hued and many folded—See, thy hand*
*Is kindled with the glowing dust of these,*[1]
*Thy maiden emblems have a heart as warm*
*As other maids who look as white as they.*
*All white is rare in aught that lives: in snow*
*We find it, but the firstlings of the snow—*
*Fair maids of February as we say—*
*Have in them, look'd to close, a spark of fire.'*

Probably the poet shrank from traducing, even through the mouth of the guilty Queen, his favourite 'February fair-maids'. But I think the lines are worth preserving.

In the 'Butcher's Book' there is, very roughly jotted down, a curious simile for which the poet never seems to have found a suitable application and which he therefore never used. No doubt the lines represent an observation made on the High Down at Farringford.

*Look, as a swallow cirles about a man,*
*Who rides or walks a down, because his feet*
*Stir up wing'd things on which it lives its life. . . .*

In the 'C' notebook occur two or three interesting passages. One describes Mark's parting from Vivien after their conversation regarding Arthur and his Knights.

*Loud laughed the graceless King*
*And like some long stilt-walker of the fens,*
*More wood than man, shambled away to bed.*

Tennyson probably omitted this vivid reminiscence of Somersby days, as being rather too farcical for its proposed context. The idea remains in a line of Isolt's in 'The Last Tournament' (Eversley, p. 362):

*For, ere I mated with my shambling king,*
*Ye twain had fallen out. . . .*

Here is another vivid line afterwards omitted as superfluous—it describes Vivien's appeal to Guinevere:

[1] I.e. the lilies.

*and on a festal day*
*While the great Queen was passing through the hall,*
*Gave one sharp shriek, clasp't hands above her head,*
*Cast herself down, knelt to the Queen and wept. . . .*

Finally, I will quote a variant of some lines which occur on *Works*, p. 382, where Vivien is watching the farewell of the Queen and Lancelot:

*That glance of theirs, but for the street, had been*
*A clinging kiss—how hand lingers in hand—*
*Bruise not the little fingers, Courtesy!*
*Let go at last! they ride away—to hawk*
*For waterfowl—Royaller game is mine.*
*For such a super-sexual sexual bond*
*As that grey cricket*[1] *chirped of at our hearth—*
*The heat and force of life all out of him—*
*Touch flax with fire—a glance will do—no more.*
*Lies, lies! for which I hate the world—and him*[2]
*That made me hate it, tho' he spake the truth—*
*Him least perchance—fool! for he wrong'd me most.*

In surveying the material illustrated in these pages, one is struck by the extraordinary variety in Tennyson's methods. In some Idylls he worked upon preliminary prose versions though this method was apparently not employed in the first four Idylls written.

Sometimes the prose version is more or less continuous and covers the whole or almost the whole of the poem, e.g. in 'The Holy Grail' and 'Balin and Balan'. Sometimes, as in 'Gareth and Lynette', 'The Coming', and 'The Passing', prose fragments are scattered amongst the fragments of verse.

Of course, it may be that for these Idylls, also, complete prose drafts were prepared, but from the way in which prose and verse are mingled, this does not seem probable.

Sometimes, as in 'The Holy Grail', Tennyson seems to have

[1] This refers to the old minstrel who had come to Mark's Court with stories of the vows of Arthur's Knights and their purity.

[2] Referring to Mark, who had made Vivien his mistress and taught her to hate and mistrust the ideals of the time.

completed the structure of the story in his head before commencing to write and then to have written the poem down as a whole.

Sometimes his fragmentary ideas are jotted down, either quite disconnectedly (the 'Enid' poems and 'Gareth and Lynette') or more or less in sequence ('Guinevere'). In one instance ('Guinevere') there are notes so rough as to be mere indications of the fleeting thought. But speaking generally the verse, even when only in fragments, has, by the time the first rough note is written, already reached, more or less, its final structure and rhythm, even where these are most elaborate; the poet's subsequent efforts being devoted to what Goethe described to Eckermann as 'that mode of altering and improving where, by continued invention, the imperfect is heightened into the perfect'. Often, it seems from the discontinuity of the writing that a poem was discontinuously perfected, the poet, with the whole story already in his mind, turning it over and over and composing it by fragments as and when the inspiration came to him, and not following it continually through its sequence. This method seems to have been adopted in some of the most successful pieces of narrative (e.g. the 'Enid' Idylls) and probably the poet was able to use the method successfully because he had already worked out the sequence of the story in his head just as carefully as he did in the case of poems, such as 'The Holy Grail', the first drafts of which were written down in a complete logical sequence.

This wide variety of technique was probably made possible by Tennyson's extraordinarily retentive memory. It mattered little to him whether the poem was on paper or in his mind only. If he wrote a story continuously it was because he had completed it in his mind in that form. If he wrote it down in scattered and discontinuous fragments it was because it came to him in that form and he knew that when he had completed it he would have no difficulty in writing it out consecutively with very little reference to his notes.

## TENNYSON AS A NARRATIVE POET

The account which I have given of the unusual methods adopted by Tennyson in composing the *Idylls* may well raise in the reader's mind the question of his status as a narrative poet.

Modern critics have not rated this very high—indeed, Mr. T. S. Eliot, who gives many of Tennyson's achievements full and generous recognition, in his essay on *In Memoriam* (*Selected Essays*, p. 331) says bluntly that Tennyson had no gift for narrative—'could not tell a story at all'. Such a statement is very difficult to prove (I will come back later to the few explanations which Mr. Eliot offers in support of it) or to disprove, but there are at least certain facts which suggest its improbability.

In childhood Tennyson used to fascinate with his stories not only his own brothers and sisters but his cousins at Bayons Manor, where the stock of the Somersby Tennysons was generally at a discount. At Cambridge and afterwards he was renowned as a raconteur, which at least suggests that he had an appreciation of the significant in character and incident and the power to express this vividly and economically. Lastly, of all his extensive output, the two most popular volumes were the *Idylls of the King* of 1859 and the *Enoch Arden* volume of 1864. It is difficult to believe that these would have had so wide an appeal or that they would have been admired as they were by Dickens and Thackeray, if the poems contained in them had not been effective as stories.

Indeed, a careful consideration of Tennyson's work shows, I submit, that he was a brilliant and singularly versatile story-teller. Leaving aside for a moment the *Idylls* and *The Princess*, one finds among his shorter pieces (the great majority of which are of course lyrical or idyllic) a remarkable range of effective experiment.

In 'The Revenge', 'The Defence of Lucknow' and 'The Charge of The Heavy Brigade' (three of the most successful Ballads in modern English literature) he showed himself fully capable of swift dramatic movement in widely varying and quite original styles. That mysterious and evocative poem 'The Lady of Shalott' (written nearly fifty years before) owes much of its effectiveness to the story which is so subtly and appealingly suggested.

In *Maud*, the poet accomplished something entirely new in the way of narrative. He told a tense and violent story entirely through the emotional reactions of the narrator, expressed in a purely lyrical form, and so subjectively that in the entire poem of about 1500 lines only one name is mentioned, that of the eponymous heroine. Whatever views may be held about the ethics or psychology of *Maud*, no one who heard Mr. Marius Goring read it over the radio can have any doubt as to its effectiveness as narrative.

Very different from all these is 'The Village Wife', published in 1880 (see above, p. 31). This describes in about 120 lines and with remarkable pungency the gradual decay and final collapse of a feckless county family, while at the same time bringing out with extraordinary brilliance the conceit, malice and ignorance of the rustic narrator. Of another rustic tale 'Dora', told in a very different manner, Wordsworth said that in it Tennyson had achieved something which he himself had been attempting all his life without success. From these examples (and others could be quoted) it certainly seems that Tennyson can claim considerable success as a story-teller on a small scale.

What of the longer poems? Mr. Eliot's argument is that Tennyson was incapable of anything less static than an 'Idyll', which he defines as 'a short poem descriptive of some picturesque scene or incident'. Tennyson's poems (including the *Idylls of the King*) are, he says, always descriptive, always picturesque, but never really narrative. *The Princess* he describes as an Idyll protracted to 'such length as to become unreadable', by which I assume that he intends to qualify the poem as a succession of descriptions of picturesque scenes or incidents. He implies that Tennyson cannot, as the great narrative poets do, 'set before you real men talking, carry you on in real events moving'. I hope I have shown that in poems of small scale Tennyson was fully capable of meeting these last-mentioned requirements. In fantasies like the *Idylls* and *The Princess*, of course, he had a harder task, but even here I think he did succeed (though no doubt with varying degrees of success) in creating the impression of real men talking and real events moving.

I would select 'Lancelot and Elaine' and 'The Holy Grail' as being pre-eminently successful in both respects—for example, in 'The Holy Grail' the conversations between Percivale and Ambrosius; the adventures of Galahad and Lancelot; the coming of the Grail and the departure of the Knights on the Quest, and the final scene with Arthur's closing speech; in 'Lancelot and Elaine', Elaine's love story, death and last voyage, and the final scenes between Lancelot and Guinevere, and Lancelot and Arthur.

If further examples are needed, I would refer to the opening scene of 'Pelleas and Ettarre', and the greater part of 'Merlin and Vivien', the dialogue between Guinevere and the little Maid in 'Guinevere' and Arthur's long march to the great battle in the West which begins 'The Passing'. The above are only a few examples and many more might be quoted.

*The Princess* is a more difficult matter—it is clear that Tennyson first intended this as a kind of burlesque, but found that the serious implications of the story ran away with him, so that it came at last, as he says himself, 'to quite a solemn close'. One cannot therefore look for the exciting narrative, the lack of which Mr. Eliot seems to lament, in the first half of the poem, although one can expect (and many people have found in *The Princess*) a lightness and charm which carries one along with a skill comparable to Pope's achievement in *The Rape of the Lock*. When, however, the poem takes a serious turn, Tennyson's art rises to the occasion, and I would claim that Cantos v and vi contain some of the best narrative verse in English.

As for 'Enoch Arden', Mr. Eliot does not specifically deal with this poem and I cannot conceive on what ground its narrative power can be questioned.

Of course, Tennyson had his own way of telling a story. Very sensibly he chose a method suitable for the development of his special gifts. Though, as I have shown, he was perfectly capable of rapid narrative, he was not particularly interested in this, and preferred a slower movement, which gave scope to his unrivalled power of creating background and atmosphere. One example of this is in the lines describing Enoch Arden's walk to his home from the port where he has been landed after his long years on the desert island.

> *. . . Bright was that afternoon,*
> *Sunny but chill; till drawn thro' either chasm,*
> *Where either haven open'd on the deeps,*
> *Roll'd a sea-haze and whelm'd the world in gray;*
> *Cut off the length of highway on before,*
> *And left but narrow breadth to left and right*
> *Of wither'd holt or tilth or pasturage.*
> *On the nigh-naked tree the robin piped*
> *Disconsolate, and thro' the dripping haze*

*The dead weight of the dead leaf bore it down;*
*Thicker the drizzle grew, deeper the gloom;*
*Last, as it seem'd, a great mist-blotted light*
*Flared on him, and he came upon the place.*

The slower movement also gave the poet time to apply his dramatic talent, which is so admirably employed, for example, in 'Merlin and Vivien', in the sixth Canto of *The Princess*, at the opening of the 'Last Tournament' and in the scene where Enoch Arden looks in through the window of Philip's house at his wife with her new husband and family. Two rather unconventional practises of the poet may be mentioned. He liked, especially in the Idylls, to begin a story with a picture or description—e.g. of Merlin with Vivien lying at his feet in the forest of Broceliande, or of Elaine gazing at Lancelot's shield in her turret chamber at Astolat—and then to work backwards in time (cf. the beginnings of 'The Marriage of Geraint', 'The Holy Grail', 'The Last Tournament' and 'Guinevere'). Also he disliked (as he said about his plays) to end his scenes with a bang—or, as he once phrased it, to leave his readers 'poised on the top of a wave'. He preferred allowing the wave to break. For example, of the Idylls only 'Merlin and Vivien' and 'Pelleas at Ettarre' can be said to finish with a strong curtain. In the other Idylls (and in 'Enoch Arden' where the last line is one of the most adversely criticized in all Tennyson's works) he preferred to end quietly with a diminuendo of emotion. Some critics have perhaps found these idiosyncrasies uncongenial, although the first is after all an application of the maxim *in medias res* and the second must often have an advantage in subtilty and refinement. It may be also that modern critics and readers miss in Tennyson the analysis and careful build-up of character which is so strong a feature of contemporary literature. That he was perfectly capable of this is clear from 'St. Simeon Stylites' and the Lincolnshire poems, but in general he preferred to concentrate on truth of emotion and sentiment, drawing his characters on broad and simple lines to fit in with and support the emotional development of the story. I have always thought the characterization of Princess Ida extraordinarily successful in this respect, for, in spite of the extravagance and even absurdity of her scheme, she stands out as a sympathetic, impressive and convincing figure. In the same way, in 'Enoch Arden', Tennyson did not attempt to build up the character of a fisherman, as he might well have done, on the lines of his Northern Farmers and Cobblers. He emphasized simply and broadly just those qualities, and only those, which were fundamental to the emotional development of the poem, loyalty, unselfishness, self-control and determination.

Perhaps a brief analysis of 'Lancelot and Elaine' may serve to draw together the threads of my argument. In this poem Tennyson handled with great skill a complicated array of material—the institution by King Arthur of the great 'Diamond Jousts' at Camelot, with the brilliantly told story of the finding of the prize jewels; the misunderstanding by Lancelot of the Queen's wishes which leads to his decision to compete in the Tournament incognito; the chance which brings Lancelot, wandering over

*the long backs of the bushless downs*

to the solitary castle of Astolat, where neither he nor the blazonings of his shield are recognized and he exchanges his own for the blank shield of Sir Torre, and agrees to wear Elaine's favour in his helmet at the Tournament for further disguise, thus, all against his own intention, confirming her dawning love for him; the great Tournament at Camelot, where Lancelot is set upon by his own kinsmen, who do not recognize him, is grievously wounded and escapes, still unrecognized, to the hermit's cave, after having been declared the winner of the diamond; Arthur's sending of the light-of-love Gawain to find the unknown victor and give him the diamond; Gawain's wanderings, which bring him to Astolat, where he discovers the identity of the victorious knight and leaves the diamond in Elaine's keeping; Elaine's discovery of the wounded and almost dying Lancelot in the hermit's cave and the devotion with which she nurses him back to health; their return to Astolat, where she declares her love for him and asks to be allowed to follow him through the world, which he perforce rejects, telling her that this is not love:

*but love's first flash in youth,*
*Most common; yea, I know it of mine own self:*
*And you yourself will smile at your own self*

N

> *Hereafter, when you yield your flower of life*
> *To one more fitly yours, not thrice your age:*
> *And then will I, for true you are and sweet*
> *Beyond mine old belief in womanhood,*
> *More specially should your good knight be poor,*
> *Endow you with broad land and territory*
> *Even to the half my realm beyond the seas,*
> *So that would make you happy: furthermore,*
> *Ev'n to the death, as tho' ye were my blood,*
> *In all your quarrels will I be your knight.*
> *This will I do, dear damsel, for your sake,*
> *And more than this I cannot.*

'of all this,' says Elaine, 'will I nothing' and is carried swooning to her tower. Next morning Lancelot leaves the castle and, urged by Elaine's father to 'use some rough discourtesy to blunt or break her passion', rides away without saying goodbye to her, although she

> *Unclasping flung the casement back, and look'd*
> *Down on his helm, from which her sleeve had gone,*
> *And Lancelot knew the little clinking sound;*
> *And she by tact of love was well aware*
> *That Lancelot knew that she was looking at him.*
> *And yet he glanced not up, nor waved his hand,*
> *Nor bad farewell, but sadly rode away.*
> *This was the one discourtesy that he used.*

Thus rebuffed by Lancelot, Elaine pines away, and, just before her death, asks that her body decked 'in all she has of rich' may be laid upon a richly decked barge and rowed by an old deaf-and-dumb servant of the house up the river to the King's Palace at Westminster, with a letter in her dead fingers addressed to Lancelot telling him that, since he left her taking no farewell, she has come to take a last farewell of him. So in due course her sad chariot bier, with her two brothers and the old man walking beside it, passes like a shadow through the summer fields, she is laid upon the barge, which moves slowly up the river into the great city where, in an oriel window at the waterside, Lancelot is kneeling to offer the Queen his tourney prize. But the Queen has heard of Elaine's love for Lancelot. Mad with jealousy, she flings the diamonds into the river and rushes from the room. A moment afterwards the funeral barge passes beneath Lancelot's eyes to the Palace steps. The Knights and ladies flock in wonder to the landing-stage. Arthur takes and reads the letter: Lancelot tells Elaine's pitiful story and Arthur orders that she shall be buried

> *not as one unknown,*
> *Not meanly, but with gorgeous obsequies,*
> *And mass, and rolling music, like a queen.*

There the wave poises, but the poet lets it break in a beautiful scene between the King and Lancelot, and the great knight is left seated on the river bank, while the barge passes slowly back down the broad stream, debating sadly in his heart whether the Queen's jealousy may not mean that her love, which has made him traitor to his King, and taken from him all hope of an innocent love such as Elaine offered him, may not be already waning:

> *'Mine own name shames me, seeming a reproach,*
> *Lancelot, whom the Lady of the Lake*
> *Caught from his mother's arms—the wondrous one*
> *Who passes thro' the vision of the night—*
> *She chanted snatches of mysterious hymns*
> *Heard on the winding waters, eve and morn*
> *She kiss'd me saying, " Thou art fair, my child,*
> *As a king's son," and often in her arms*
> *She bare me, pacing on the dusky mere.*
> *Would she had drown'd me in it, where'er it be!*
> *For what am I? what profits me my name*
> *Of greatest knight? I fought for it, and have it:*
> *Pleasure to have it, none; to lose it, pain;*
> *Now grown a part of me: but what use in it?*
> *To make men worse by making my sin known?*
> *Or sin seem less, the sinner seeming great?*
> *Alas for Arthur's greatest knight, a man*
> *Not after Arthur's heart! I needs must break*
> *These bonds that so defame me: not without*
> *She wills it: would I, if she will'd it? nay,*
> *Who knows? but if I would not, then may God,*
> *I pray him, send a sudden Angel down*

*To seize me by the hair and bear me far,*
*And fling me deep in that forgotten mere,*
*Among the tumbled fragments of the hills'.*
*So groan'd Sir Lancelot in remorseful pain,*
*Not knowing he should die a holy man.*

I do not see how anyone can read Tennyson's story without feeling that he managed his material with consummate skill. The whole texture is richly wrought as a mille-fleurs tapestry, but this only serves to heighten the tragedy of Elaine's innocent passion and she remains the centre of the picture from the opening lines, which show her sitting in her turret chamber poring over the shield of the unknown knight, until the empty barge, oared by the dumb old servitor, passes slowly homeward down the river. The characters are drawn with broad and telling strokes, and the brilliant descriptions of Palace, tournament, castle and hermit's cave add life and visual reality to the whole.

But for the consideration of Tennyson's narrative power it is perhaps most valuable to compare his version of the story with that of Malory (Bk. XVIII) from which its main outlines are taken. Such a comparison reveals that Tennyson's omissions, additions and alterations were made with the greatest skill. The device of beginning the story with the picture of Elaine poring over the unknown knight's shield is, of course, pure Tennyson. So is the description of Arthur's finding of the diamonds and Lancelot's desire to win them as a present for the Queen. In Malory Arthur knows that Lancelot is competing in the Tournament, and there is no very clear reason for his going to it disguised. Tennyson makes this a telling episode in the guilty understanding between Lancelot and the Queen. Tennyson (inevitably) omits Malory's catalogue of knights and combats at the Tournament and substitutes one of his most concise and vivid descriptions. He elaborates most effectively the description of Elaine's tendance of the wounded Lancelot and improves Malory's description of the parting between them by the addition of the episode of Lancelot's one discourtesy. Very important indeed are Tennyson's additions at the end of the story. The scene between Lancelot and Guinevere in the oriel window is one of these, and so are the very beautiful conversation between Lancelot and

Arthur after the burial and Lancelot's final soliloquy. In addition, Tennyson cut out some unnecessary incidents (such as Lancelot's premature effort to take horse and arms when recovering from his wound), and he fined down many of Malory's episodes which unduly hold up the story, strengthening this by expanding others, for example (in addition to those which I have already mentioned) the account of Lancelot's sojourn at the Castle of Astolat, with his stirring account of King Arthur's battles against the Heathen, and the descriptions of Guinevere's jealousy and Gawain's visit to Astolat.

In fact, from the point of view of pure story-telling I would maintain that every alteration which Tennyson made to Malory's narrative is a definite improvement. If this is true, it will surely be admitted that the man who could so improve on one of the finest stories of one of our greatest story-tellers cannot have been entirely without talent as a story-teller himself.

It may be said that 'Lancelot and Elaine' succeeds as a story because so much of it is taken from Malory. In reply to this I would point out that 'The Holy Grail', which seems to me no less successful as narrative, is almost entirely original, very little being taken from Malory or elsewhere.

There remains the question whether Tennyson was one of those rare beings who had the capacity to write a great continuous epic story. This must always remain a matter of opinion, for he never attempted the feat—possibly because he realized that it was not suited to his genius. I have, however, in describing the composition of the Idylls, shown how skilfully he wove a connecting thread through the separate episodes and with what art he grouped these episodes round and made them illustrate the main theme of the rise and fall of the Round Table. Although, therefore, one cannot definitely assert that Tennyson could have created a great epic narrative, one cannot, I venture to submit, definitely assert the contrary.

# VI

# *On Reading Tennyson*

IN ORDER to get the best out of Tennyson's verse it is essential that it should be read aloud. This is no doubt true of most of the nineteenth-century poets (even of much of Browning's verse), but in no other poet are sound and rhythm so intimately and deliberately expressive.

Tennyson read his own poems aloud with inimitable effect, and it is possible from the accounts of those who heard him read and from cylindrical phonograph records[1] of his reading, made for Edison in 1890, to form a fairly good impression of the methods which he adopted.

The first thing to remember is that Tennyson's poems, whether sentimental, tragic, lyrical or humorous, were intensely felt, and he himself read them with great intensity. The phonograph records provide very powerful evidence of this and there is plenty of written evidence to the same effect. Edward FitzGerald spoke of the terrific rendering of *Oriana* that he used to give at Cambridge dinner-tables, and D. G. Rossetti left an account of an evening in 1855 when Tennyson, a few weeks after the publication of *Maud*, read the poem from beginning to end, sitting on the sofa in Rossetti's rooms in Chatham Street, with one leg

[1] These records made by the poet when he was over eighty and had only just recovered from a severe illness were made in wax and could only be played on an old-fashioned phonograph. Moreover, with the lapse of time and inadequate care in maintenance, they had largely perished when they were discovered thirty years ago. When first made they must have been extremely impressive, for the power of the renderings is still very evident and they covered a wide range of his poems, including, for example, several of his most famous short lyrics and excerpts from *Maud*, the Wellington 'Ode', the 'Northern Farmer, New Style,' and 'Boadicea'. Obviously these records provide most important evidence of the principles according to which the poet wished his poems to be read, and, as I am fortunate enough to have had the chance of studying them all at various times, I include my inferences from them in this essay.

drawn up under him and the book held close to his short-sighted eyes, the party, which included Robert and Elizabeth Browning, not breaking up until half-past two in the morning. Rossetti recorded that 'whilst the fiery passages were delivered with a voice and vehemence which Tennyson alone of living men could compass, the softer passages and the songs made the tears course down his cheeks'. Some poems he felt so intensely that he could never read them to an audience; this applied particularly to *In Memoriam*.[1] Anyone who reads Tennyson aloud today, therefore, must be prepared to 'let himself go'. There is, however, a very important qualification. As I have said, rhythm and sound are essential elements of expression in Tennyson's poems, and dramatic expression must never be allowed to override these—it must rather speak through them. In this (and every other) respect Mr. Marius Goring's recent broadcast reading of *Maud* was remarkably successful, bearing in mind that on the air, where the reader is not visible to his audience, he must, to make his points effective, use a rather more normal dramatic method than when contact between reader and audience is more immediate. It follows that the stronger and more insistent the rhythm, the more dramatic emphasis can be used without overriding it, and, as I have said, I believe that Tennyson chose very strongly marked metres for many of his poems, particularly those in the Lincolnshire dialect, in order that the reader might be able to use the utmost dramatic freedom without overpowering the rhythm. His own rendering of 'The Northern Farmer' for the phonograph was delightfully free—almost as one might imagine Mr. Stanley Holloway reading it. I think he chose similarly strong rhythms for intensely dramatic ballads like 'Rizpah' and 'Despair' for the same reason. 'Rizpah' he himself read with extraordinary power and abandon—'Bones' he used to call it with grim affection.

Much of what I have written about Tennyson's versification is relevant to the subject of this essay, especially the pages about the blank verse. So far as both rhythm and sound are concerned the principles applied in all his verse are similar. The most important

[1] There is only one reference to his reading from this poem aloud and that was on the occasion of Henry Hallam's death. After hearing the news of this, Tennyson on several successive evenings read aloud to his wife the sections of the poem which had meant most to Arthur's father.

sound element is the broad vowel; and here one must remember that Tennyson was a North Countryman, who never acquired the more clipt and mincing pronunciation of the South, but retained all his life traces of the Lincolnshire accent, with which he had been familiar in his youth. He achieved a great variety of sound with the vowel 'a'. Before a consonant he used the light North Country pronunciation—'dănce', not 'darnce'; for example:

*But follow, let the torrent dănce thee down.*

Here 'darnce' would entirely spoil the effect, which must be light and rapid like the torrent. Sometimes the effect aimed at is visual:

*Roared as when the roaring breakers boom and blănch on the precipices.*

Here the light 'a' in 'blănch' is essential to suggest the whiteness of the breaking wave.

'A' before a consonant followed by another 'e' and in such diphthongs as 'ay' and 'ai' Tennyson pronounced rather broadly with open lips (e.g. 'paagent', not 'padgent'), thus enabling the vowel to be held:

*The long light shāākes across the lāākes.*

*Let the great river tāāke me to the māin.*

Here the long vowel sounds are essential to the full melody of the lines.

'O', Tennyson pronounced long where he could; 'knolledge' he particularly abhorred.

*Knōwledge comes but wisdom lingers.*

'Knolledge' would ruin the line. He even said 'shōne' and not 'shonn' (in 'Despair', Stanza III, he rhymes 'shone' with 'own'), though I do not think he said 'gōne', nor do I know whether there is any etymological basis for his practice. Confirmation of Tennyson's treatment of these vowels comes from the description of the poet in the Prologue to *Morte d'Arthur*, who read:

*Mouthing out his hollow oes and aes.*

He could, however, use muted sounds with great effect—as, for example, in the opening of the Wellington Ode:

*Bury the great duke—*

a line which Edward FitzGerald criticized, saying that so great a poem ought to have opened with broad sonorous vowels. He did not realize that Tennyson deliberately used the muted vowels to indicate the dull tramp of the funeral cortège.

Two more small points before I pass to another subject. Frequently, but perhaps not invariably, Tennyson pronounced 'ue' in 'true' and similar words almost as 'ewe'. This would give a variation of sound from the normal pronunciation 'oo', and the reader may employ it if he thinks fit.

The name of a favourite plant, woodbine, he pronounced 'woodbin'—possibly a Lincolnshire survival:

*And the woodbin(e) spices are wafted abroad.*

Here a long 'i' would spoil the line.

With consonants there is little scope for variations in pronunciation, but some special points may be noted. Tennyson pronounced his 'r's' with a good strong roll. This was particularly noticeable, I remember, in the line from *The Princess* which I have quoted above:

*Let the grreat rriverr take me to the main.*

He particularly disliked the recurrent 's' sound in English and eliminated it as much as he could. 'Kicking the geese out of the boat', he called this practice. Where, therefore, there is a considerable use of the letter 's', the reader may be sure that this was done with a purpose, and the 's' sound should be emphasized in reading. The purpose is sometimes extremely subtle; for example, in *The Princess* (Canto VII):

*But cease to move so near the Heavens, and cease*
*To glide a sunbeam by the blasted Pine,*
*To sit a star upon the sparkling spire;*

the last line is obviously intended to suggest the cold sparkle of a solitary ice-peak high up in the Alps. And in *In Memoriam*, LXXXVI:

*. . . let the fancy fly*
*From belt to belt of crimson seas*
*On leagues of odour streaming far,*
*To where in yonder orient star*
*A hundred spirits whisper 'Peace.'*

The last three words suggest the idea of a remote whispering sound.

But although the consonants have not the same importance in Tennyson's verse as the vowels, his use of consonants was equally purposeful.

Alliteration he did not much care for, not using it freely even in his imitations of the old Anglo-Saxon alliterative verse (see above, p. 143). Indeed, he found that alliteration came too easily and often had laboriously to remove it from his first drafts. He did not often use it for heightening the tension of his effects, as Manley Hopkins did so skilfully. Much less did he let it run riot, as Swinburne was apt to do. He evidently regarded alliteration as rather a clumsy method of obtaining emphasis. Examples of its use can, however, be found—as, for instance, the well-known lines in *Morte d'Arthur*:

*The bare black cliff clanged round him, as he based*
*His feet on juts of slippery crag that rang*
*Sharp-smitten with the dint of armed heels—*

Here the alliteration of 'b's' and 'c's' in the first line is much helped by the clanging vowel sounds, 'bare', 'black', 'clanged'.

Another famous example comes from 'Lancelot and Elaine':

*His honour rooted in dishonour stood,*
*And faith unfaithful kept him falsely true.*

And another in 'Tears, Idle Tears':

*Tears from the depth of some divine despair.*

Sometimes the poet used a double alliteration, as in 'God and the Universe':

*Must my day be dark by reason, oh ye Heavens, of your endless nights;*
*Rush of suns, and roll of systems, and your fiery clash of meteorites?*

But, in general, he preferred to get his effects by 'assonance': that is to say, by repeating consonants and vowels at some distance, so as to get an echo and patterned repetition of sound. A striking example of this is the short lyric, 'Frater ave atque Vale'.[1]

*Frater Ave atque Vale*

*Row us out from Desenzano, to your Sirmione row!*
*So they row'd, and there we landed—'O venusta Sirmio!'*
*There to me thro' all the groves of olive in the summer glow,*
*There beneath the Roman ruin where the purple flowers grow,*
*Came that 'Ave atque Vale' of the Poet's hopeless woe,*
*Tenderest of Roman poets nineteen hundred years ago,*
*'Frater Ave atque Vale'—as we wander'd to and fro*
*Gazing at the Lydian laughter of the Garda Lake below*
*Sweet Catullus's all-but-island, olive-silvery Sirmio!*

In reading this poem the recurrence of the letters 'r', 'l', 'v', 'o' and 'a' binds the lines together and gives the poem a musical form which should be delicately emphasized in reading. Countless similar examples are to be found in Tennyson's poems, whether narrative, lyric or elegiac, and he often used his control of sound and rhythm for more definite ends than the production of melody. For example, the third of these lines from 'The Gardener's Daughter' describing the long-drawn onset of night:

*. . . or as once we met*
*Unheedful, tho' beneath a whispering rain*
*Níght slíd dówn óne lóng stréam of sighing wind*
*And on her bosom bore the baby sleep.*

or these lines from *Maud*, Section XVIII, 1, the second of which is intended to give a light tripping effect:

*Just now the dry-tongued laurels pattering talk*
*Seémed hér líght stép along the terrace walk.*

Then there are some lines in 'To E.L. on his travels in Greece'

[1] This poem is imaginatively analysed in Harold Nicholson's *Tennyson*, pp. 285-6.

which exquisitely suggest the lazy water rising and falling in the Naiad's cave:

> *. . . on the swell*
> *The sílver líly heáved and féll.*

Another famous example is the opening of the fourth stanza of 'The Charge of the Light Brigade', where vowel sound, assonance and rhythm combine vividly to picture the gleam and sweep of the sword play:

> *Flásh'd all their sabres bare*
> *Flásh'd as they turn'd in air. . . .*

Equally vivid is the description in 'The Defence of Lucknow' of the receding echoes of the exploded mine:

> *Soón as the blást of their únderground thúnderclap écho'd awáy.*

More subtle are the lines in the Wellington Ode describing the fruitless French charges at Waterloo:

> *Dash'd on every rocky square*
> *Their súrging chárges foám'd themselves awáy,*

and those at the close of 'The Charge of the Heavy Brigade', which depict the breaking of the Russian line before the final impact of the English reserves:

> *For our men gallopt up with a cheer and a shout*
> *And the foemen surged, and waver'd, and reel'd*
> *Úp the hill, úp the hill, úp the hill, oút of the fiéld,*
> *And óver the brów and awáy.*

One particularly subtle example occurs in 'Oenone' (*Works*, p. 40):

> *The gorges, opening wide apart, reveal*
> *Troas and Ilion's column'd citadel*
> *The crown of Troas.*

Here in the first line the vowels in the second, third, fourth and fifth words which require a gradually wider opening of the mouth to pronounce them, suggest the gradual opening of the gorge, and the sharp, clear sound of 'reveal' brings suddenly before the mind's eye the distant vision of the divinely built city of Ilion far away on the plain.

Perhaps the most brilliant descriptive use of rhythm, vowel sound, assonance and alliteration is to be found in the closing lines of 'The Revenge':

*When a wínd from the lánds they had ruin'd awóke from sleep,*
*And the wáter began to heáve and the weather to móan,*
*And or éver that évening énded a greát gále bléw,*
*And a wáve like the wáve that is raísed by an eárthquake gréw,*
*Till it smóte on their húlls and their saíls and their másts and their flágs,*
*And the whóle séa plungéd and féll on the shót-shatter'd návy of Spáin,*
*And the líttle Revénge hersélf went dówn by the ísland crágs*
*To be lóst evermóre in the máin.*

A strongly contrasting device which Tennyson occasionally uses is the repetition of the same rhythm over a series of lines to produce a cumulative effect; a good example of this occurs in 'Guinevere', where Arthur recalls to the Queen the nature of the vows which he imposed on his Knights:

*To break the heathen and uphold the Christ,*
*To ride abroad redressing human wrongs,*
*To speak no slander, no, nor listen to it,*
*To honour his own word as if his God's*
*To lead sweet lives in purest chastity,*
*To love one maiden only, cleave to her,*
*And worship her by years of noble deeds,*
*Until they won her; . . .*

Other telling examples occur in the lines which I have quoted on p. 57 above from the Epilogue to the *Idylls of the King* and those at the end of the Dedication to the Prince Consort:

*May all love,*
*His love, unseen but felt, o'ershadow Thee!*
*The love of all thy sons encompass Thee,*
*The love of all thy daughters cherish Thee,*
*The love of all thy people comfort Thee,*
*Till God's love set Thee at his side again!*

In 'The Brook' he uses the same device for describing the 'long long-winded tale' of the old farmer (quoted on p. 15 above). In reading, this regular recurrence of the rhythm should be emphasized.

In contrast to these repetitive paragraphs are the long continuous verse paragraphs, which should be read as far as possible without pausing to draw breath. Tennyson had phenomenal lung power and enjoyed reading such passages and in making others read them. For example, he delighted in getting people who prided themselves on their skill in reading to attempt Section LXXXVI of *In Memoriam* (see p. 138 above), which consists of four stanzas with no stops except a few commas and needs to be read in one continuous sweep. The last eight-line stanza of 'Come into the Garden, Maud', he would read (as the phonograph records show) at full lung-pressure and without a single pause, rising towards the end on a tremendous *crescendo*, and letting the last two lines run down in a kind of torrential passion which I have found quite inimitable. In the refrain of the bugle song also he used a dying fall which it is very difficult to reproduce:

*Blow bugle, answer echo, dying, dying, dying.*

Another habit of his goes entirely against the usual canons of reading. He liked to drop a note in the penultimate syllable or the last syllable but two of the line—thus assimilating his reading even more strongly to a dramatic chant.

Another idiosyncrasy was what he called his 'ghost voice', a kind of vibrant whisper, which he used for certain poems, such, for example, as 'Break, Break' and the shell lyric in *Maud*. Another was the raising of the key in certain passages of the Wellington Ode which I have described in the note on p. 139 above. A modern reader may well feel shy of such idiosyncrasies, but they are evidence of the importance which Tennyson attached to the music of his verse. Reading it was to him as much music as drama, and no interpretation which does not give both elements their full value can carry out his intentions.

Finally, to show how Tennyson could apply the full range of his poetic technique to convey, through lines which seem starkly simple, an infinity of meaning and suggestion, aural, visual and spiritual, I will quote the opening stanzas of 'Crossing the Bar', which he himself wished always to be placed at the end of his collective works:

*Sunset and evening star,*
*And one clear call for me!*
*And may there be no moaning of the bar,*
*When I put out to sea,*

*But such a tide as moving seems asleep,*
*Too full for sound or foam,*
*When that which drew from out the boundless deep*
*Turns again home.*

If one reads these lines slowly, giving rhythm, vowel sounds and initial consonants full weight, it is easy to see how they have become perhaps the most famous in all Tennyson's poetry.